MY
EPIC
DOODLETASTIC
BIBLE
STORYBOOK

ZONDERKIDZ

My Epic, Doodletastic Storybook Bible
Copyright © 2020, 2023 by Bob Hartman
Ilustrations © 2020 by Gareth Williams

First published in Great Britain in 2020 as *The Link-It-Up Bible*

Requests for information should be addressed to:

Zonderkidz, 3900 *Sparks Dr. SE, Grand Rapids, Michigan 49546*

ISBN 978-0-310-14221-8

Zondervan titles may be purchased in bulk for educational, business, fundraising, or sales promotional
use. For information, please email SpecialMarkets@Zondervan.com.

Zonderkidz is a trademark of Zondervan.

Interior design: Gareth Williams

Printed in the United States of America

23 24 25 26 27 28 / LSC / 10 9 8 7 6 5 4 3 2 1

MY EPIC, DOODLETASTIC BIBLE STORYBOOK

60 BIBLE STORIES TO READ, COLOR, AND DRAW

ZONDERkidz

Contents

OLD TESTAMENT

OLD TESTAMENT

THE CREATION STORY

AT FIRST, there was **GOD THE FATHER**. At first, there was **GOD THE SON**. At first, there was **GOD THE SPIRIT**. And that's all there was. Then God said, "**LIGHT**,"  and there was day and there was **NIGHT**. And that's all there was. But there was more, so much more to come...So God said, "**SEA**" and "**SKY**" and "**SPACE**." And there were WAVES FLOWING and clouds blowing and galaxies GROWING.

And that's all there was. But there was more, so much more to come...

So God said, "**EARTH**," and the waters parted...

WHAT OTHER BIBLE STORY HAS WATERS THAT PART?

...and mountains started and flat plateaus and hollowed valleys followed.

And that's all there was. But there was more, so much more to come...

So God said, "**PLANTS**," and fields FLOWERED and meadows spread and forests full of trees burst forth. And that's all there was. But there

was more, so much more to come…So God said, "**SUN**" and God said,

"**MOON**" and God said, "**STARS**" and gifted the days and the nights

with light. And that's all there was. But there was more, so much more

to come…So God said, "**FISH**," like a spoken {wish}, and up through the

waves they leapt, deep down into the seas they *DIVED,*

and all through the RIVERS they *raced.* And that's all there was. But there

was more, so much more to come…So God said, "**BIRDS**,"

HI!

and their wings split the {air} their feet fixed on branches, and

their cries filled the skies. And that's all

THAT'S ROARSOME!

there was. But there was more, so much more to

come…So God said, "**ANIMALS**," and the jungles and

the forests and the plains embraced the chasing and racing life that

started, with a startle, among them. And that's all there was. Beautiful and

AMAZING as it was. But there was more, so much more to come...So God

made **YOU**. Well, a WOMAN like you or a MAN like you.

And like him too. Made in his image...

Q. WHO ELSE IS MADE IN THE IMAGE OF GOD?
HINT: WE CELEBRATE HIS BIRTHDAY AT CHRISTMAS...

Made to make. Made to LOVE. Made to take care of all there was. And

even though God rested when he was done, it was only for a while. For his

story and our story tell us there was MORE, so much more to come...→

HIDE-AND-SEEK WITH GOD

What came next? Something sad. **GOD** planted a **GARDEN**, a

 perfect place, for the first man, ADAM, and the

first woman, EVE, to call home. But a **SERPENT**

lived there too—the craftiest creature God had made. So the serpent

sidled up to Eve one day, as she stood with Adam next to the Tree of the

Knowledge of **GOOD** and **EVIL**. "Did God really say that you

TREE OF KNOWLEDGE

must not eat fruit from the trees in this **BEAUTIFUL** garden, this garden

of Eden?" he asked. "Of course not," Eve replied. "We are allowed to eat

FRUIT from **EVERY** tree. Well, apart from the Knowledge TREE, this

one in the middle of the garden." And then she bent down and whispered, "For

DO NOT EAT

God says that if we eat from this tree, we will die." "Die?" the serpent

"Don't be ridiculous! You won't die. **GOD** doesn't want you to eat the

 fruit because he knows that, if you do,

you will know what he knows—good and

evil—and then you will be just like him!" "**HMM**," Eve thought. "If the

fruit tastes as good as it looks, it has to be worth a try. And if it makes

me wise as well..." And that's when she took a bite. And that's when

she passed it to Adam and he took a bite too. And

that's when they noticed something they had

never noticed before. They were NAKED!

More than that, they were ashamed that they were naked. So they sewed

themselves some clothes out of fig leaves. And

 when they heard the (sound) of God walking in

the **GARDEN** that evening, they hid from

him among the trees. "Where are you?" God called.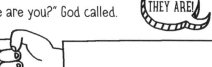

"WE'RE HIDING!" Adam called back. (He'd never hidden before and hadn't quite gotten the hang of it.) "I heard you walking in the GARDEN and I was naked. So I was afraid." "How did you know you were naked?" asked God, sadly. "You have **EATEN** the fruit from the tree, haven't you?" "It was the woman's fault!" Adam protested, pointing at Eve. "The woman you gave me!"

"The serpent tricked me!" Eve replied, pointing at the serpent.

OUCH!

"That's why I ate the fruit." "**SERPENT**," God said, "you will be CURSED above every living creature. You shall crawl on your belly. You and the woman will be enemies. And even though you will **ONE** day bruise the heel of one of her children, he will **CRUSH YOUR HEAD**." "Woman," God went on to say, "childbirth will be painful. And your husband will rule over you. And as for you, Adam," God concluded, "you will have to GROW your own food from now on. And it won't be easy. You'll have to **HACK** and **DIG**

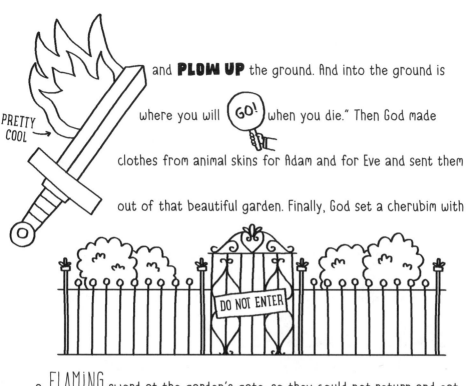

PRETTY COOL →

and **PLOW UP** the ground. And into the ground is where you will GO! when you die." Then God made clothes from animal skins for Adam and for Eve and sent them out of that beautiful garden. Finally, God set a cherubim with

DO NOT ENTER

a FLAMING sword at the garden's gate, so they could not return and eat from the **TREE OF LIFE** and live forever. But that was not the end of the story. There was more, so much **MORE** to come. There was that **PROMISE**. Of a child. Who would one day crush the serpent's head and defeat him once and for all...

UH-OH!

ANY IDEA WHO THIS CHILD MIGHT BE?

ONE ARK AND ONE MASSIVE STORM

When God made the **WORLD**, he made it beautiful. He carved a safe space,

a PERFECT place, between the chaos of the rainy waters above and the

ocean waters below, where women and men could **LIVE** and LOVE

and **FLOURISH**. But the first man and the first woman disobeyed him.

One of their sons killed the other. And, as time passed, men and

women listened less to **GOD** and more to their own selfish hearts. They did

TERRIBLE things to one another and made a messy chaos not only of

the world God had given them but of their lives as well. Things got so bad

that God was sorry he had made men and women. So he decided to start

all over again. He FOUND one good man called NOAH and told him to

build a really BIG boat: an ark. "Men and women have turned the beautiful world I made for them into a violent mess," he told Noah. "So I am going to allow the chaos of the rainy waters above and the ocean waters below to come together again in a **GREAT** flood, and destroy all life on earth.

Only you and your family—and the animals you bring with you on the ARK—will survive." So Noah and his family built the ark. And Noah and his family **GATHERED** together a pair of every animal on earth, including 7 pairs of animals that God would one day tell his people were "clean"—that is, okay for them to eat. And when everyone was on board,

God shut the door and the rain began to fall. For

forty DAYS and NIGHTS, the rain fell. For forty

days and nights, the oceans burst their banks

and swelled to meet the watery chaos from above. And the beautiful,

orderly place that **GOD** had carved out for men and women between the

waters was washed away, along with the violent chaos they had made of

their lives. But God did not **FORGET** Noah and his **FAMILY**. And, through

them, he did not forget the people or the world he had made. So he sent

a wind to BLOW. Then he shut both the windows of heaven and the ocean

fountains he had unleashed to flood the earth. And the

ark came to rest on a MOUNTAIN. For a long time, Noah

waited, sending out a raven and then a dove to see if there was a place

for them to land. And when the dove returned a second time with an

OLIVE BRANCH in her mouth, Noah knew that the waters had

subsided. Seven days LATER, the dove did not return, so

Noah and his family and all the animals came out of the ark. Just as God had done with the first **MAN** and **WOMAN**, he commanded Noah and his family to have babies and fill the earth with **LIFE**. Then he drew a rainbow onto the sky, a sign of his PROMISE that he would never flood the whole **EARTH** like that again.

GOD'S BIG PROMISE

God did not forget his **PROMISES**. His rainbow promise or that other promise either—the promise to send a child to crush the serpent, to defeat what was **WRONG** and put things **RIGHT** again. There was more, so much **MORE** to come! And this is where it started. There was a man called Abram, who lived in a place called **HARAN**. One day God spoke to **ABRAM**, and what God said was, "Follow me. Leave your country, Abram.

Leave your relatives, Abram. Leave the land of your father, Abram. And FOLLOW me to a land that I will show you." God gave Abram no maps. God gave Abram no

DIRECTIONS. Abram had no clue where he was going. But he

did have a promise. "If you follow me," God said, "I will take your children

and make a GREAT nation out of them. I will protect you. I will bless you. And

from your family I will bring a blessing to every family in the world." It

was a **BIG** promise. But the most

thing about it was that Abram had no children. And he was

already seventy-five years old, with a wife not that much

younger. So what did Abram do? He **TRUSTED** God.

He believed that amazing PROMISE. And he took his

wife and his family and everything he owned and set

off on a journey to **"WHO-KNOWS-WHERE."** God knew, of course.

THIS WAY
THAT WAY
OVER HERE

THAT'S PRETTY OLD!

And when Abram and his family arrived at last in a land called CANAAN,

God said, "This is the place. A **NEW HOME** for you and your

children!" So Abram built an altar there and gave thanks to God. There were

 BAA!

still no children, however. And as time passed and Abram

and his wife, **SARAI**, grew even older, no children

arrived. God blessed Abram, to be sure, with BIGGER

flocks of sheep and goats and cattle. And with more and more MOO!

land. But still no children. Not one. And Abram, quite understandably,

was puzzled. One night, while Abram was in his tent, God came

to him in a vision. "Fear not, Abram," God said. "I am still here—

like a shield to **PROTECT YOU**. You will get everything

I promised you." "But, Lord," Abram replied, "I still have no children!

I mean, there is this distant relative, **ELIEZER**, who I can pass

my inheritance on to..." "No," God said. "Not him. Your own child will be

your heir. Trust me. And step outside the tent for a moment." So Abram

followed God again—a much shorter **JOURNEY** this time.

He stepped outside his tent. It was a cloudless night.

"Look up at the sky," God said. "Look up and count the stars."

The sky was filled with them, too many for anyone

to count. "Your descendants, Abram—your

CHILDREN and **GRANDCHILDREN**

and **GREAT-GRANDCHILDREN** and

all who will come after them—will outnumber even

the stars in the sky. So trust me, Abram." And what did Abram do? In the

same way that he had left his home for an unknown destination, he trusted

God and **BELIEVED** that there was more, so much MORE to come. And

that God's promise would one day come true. ✳

❓❓ THREE MYSTERIOUS VISITORS ❓❓

Abram **WAITED** and **WAITED**—

HELLO, MY NAME IS

ABRAHAM

waited for God's promise to come true. He waited so

long, in FACT , that there was even time for God to CHANGE his name.

"Your name will no longer be Abram (which means **EXALTED FATHER**),"

God said, "but ABRAHAM (which means **FATHER OF NATIONS**)."

And while he was at it, God also changed the name of Abraham's wife from Sarai

(which means Princess) to Sarah (**MOTHER OF NATIONS**). They were

small changes. But they had a very BIG meaning, for they were yet another

sign that God meant to on his promise. And then,

years or so after Abraham had left his homeland and followed God to the land

of CANAAN , Abraham had **THREE** visitors. His tent was pitched

TREE-MENDOUS!

in the shade of the oaks of Mamre. But it was midday

and so it was hot. **VERY HOT!**

The arrival of those visitors was

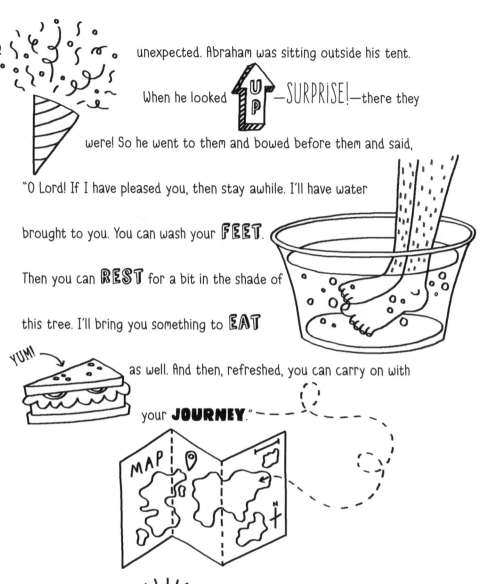

unexpected. Abraham was sitting outside his tent.

When he looked **UP**—SURPRISE!—there they

were! So he went to them and bowed before them and said,

"O Lord! If I have pleased you, then stay awhile. I'll have water

brought to you. You can wash your **FEET**.

Then you can **REST** for a bit in the shade of

this tree. I'll bring you something to **EAT**

YUM!

as well. And then, refreshed, you can carry on with

your **JOURNEY**."

MAP

Now, Abraham's speech sounds just a little unusual, doesn't it? He was talking

to **THREE** visitors, but it sounds as if he was TALKING to just **ONE**. And he

called the visitor "Lord," which makes it sound as if he was talking to someone royal. Or...maybe even...**GOD!** The thing is, Abraham had talked to God many

times. And if anyone knew what the **VOICE** of God sounded like,

it was him. So Abraham *HURRIED* into the tent

(as quickly as a ninety-nine-year-old

man can hurry!). "Sarah!" he said to his

wife. "We need flour. Lots of it! And you need to bake some cakes!" Then he

ran (at "old man" speed once again) to where his herd

of cattle was grazing. He chose the **BEST** calf he could find

and ordered a servant to kill it and cook it. And

when everything was prepared, he served the cakes and

cooked-up calf to the visitors with a heaping helping of curds and milk.

YUM! Milk As the visitors ate, they asked, "Where is your wife,

Sarah?" "In the tent," replied Abraham, matter-of-factly. "Well," said the

visitors, "by this time next year, Sarah will have given BIRTH

to a son." Now, Sarah was not just in the tent. She was

WHAT?!

listening at the tent door. "Is an old woman like me, a woman nearly ninety, really going to give birth to a child?" she wondered out loud. And then she **LAUGHED**. "Why did Sarah question what we said?" the visitors asked Abraham. "And why did she laugh? Nothing is **IMPOSSIBLE** for God! We will return in a year and by then she will have a son." When Sarah realized that

HE'S BEHIND YOU! the visitors had heard her, she was AFRAID. "I didn't laugh!" she said. "Oh yes you did!" the visitors replied. And they would have gone back and forth like that had the visitors not departed. A year passed and, just as promised, Sarah did indeed give birth to a son. And what did she call him? "LAUGHTER," of course. For that is what his name, **ISAAC**, means. But there was more.

Of course there was. A whole family to come— through whom that special child would one day be born.

A DIFFICULT SACRIFICE

Abraham had a son—the beginning of the **GREAT** nation God had promised would come from him! Isaac grew from a TODDLER to a BOY to a young MAN. And then, one day, God spoke again to Abraham. "I want you to go to the land of **MORIAH**," God said. "Build an altar there and sacrifice Isaac, the son you love." Abraham didn't know what to think. After all the waiting and all the trusting and all those years, the PROMISE had finally come true. And now God

wanted him to kill his son and the promise along with him?

Still, Abraham trusted God. And that **TRUST** had brought him this far. "God can do anything," he thought. "Even raise a man from the dead. Perhaps that is what he plans to do for Isaac."

So, early the next morning, Abraham put a saddle on his

donkey and cut WOOD for the sacrifice fire. Then,

along with two of his servants, he traveled with Isaac to

the land of Moriah. It took them **3** days. And when the

place God had chosen for the **SACRIFICE** was finally in view, Abraham

told his servants to stay with the donkey. He loaded the wood onto Isaac's

back. He grabbed a **FLAMING** torch with one hand and a knife with

the other. And off they went, father and son. As they walked, Isaac

asked a question. A question that tore at Abraham's HEART. "We have

the fire and the wood, Father. But where is the lamb for the sacrifice?"

THAT'S A LOT TO CARRY!

TWEET!

THIS STORY HAS SEVERAL THINGS IN COMMON WITH THE EVENTS WE REMEMBER AT EASTER TIME.

"God will provide the lamb, my son," the old man whispered, then walked

silently on. When they REACHED the place that God had chosen,

Abraham built an altar out of stone. He took the wood from Isaac's back

and stacked it on the stones. Then he took Isaac, tied him up,

and laid him on top of the wood. One can only IMAGINE the

frightened thoughts that must have raced through Isaac's head. And

then, as if to answer the worst of those thoughts, Abraham raised the knife

above his son. That's when he heard a VOICE —a voice from heaven.

"Do not hurt the boy!" God's angel cried. "God knows now that you

truly HONOR him and put your trust in him alone, for you were willing to

give him your only son." Abraham looked up and in front of him was a ram, its

horns caught in a thicket. So Abraham took hold of the ram, untied

his son, and offered the ram as a sacrifice instead.

Then he called the place where he had built the

altar "GOD WILL PROVIDE." And that's when the

angel spoke again, his words an ECHO of what was, by now, a familiar

promise. "Because you were willing to give God your son, God will bless you.

And your descendants will OUTNUMBER the stars in the sky and the grains

of sand at the side of the sea!" And so the promise came

true as, little by little, the family GREW ...

A HAIRY MOMENT

Isaac married a woman called **REBEKAH**. They had two children, twins in fact: **ESAU** and **JACOB**. Esau was born first, covered all over in red hair. And Jacob came right behind, with one hand grasping his OLDER brother's heel. It was a SIGN of the troubles to come—troubles that Jacob and Rebekah had a "hand" in as well. Isaac's favorite was Esau. He was hairy and BIG and STRONG. A hunter. Rebekah, however, favored

NICE TENT!

Jacob, who liked to stay indoors. Well, in-tent, actually. One day, Jacob was in the tent, cooking a lentil stew. Esau

JACOB'S LENTIL STEW

RUSHED in from the fields, famished. "Give me some of that stew!" Esau **DEMANDED**. And Jacob saw a chance to grab hold of something that Esau owned. Something that Jacob wanted badly. Esau was due to inherit the birthright—the right of the firstborn—to rule the family when Isaac died. More than that, he was due to receive the

promise God had given to Abraham and then passed on to Isaac.

 So Jacob GRINNED and ladled out a bowlful and said, "I'd

be happy to give you some stew...if you will give me your

BIRTHRIGHT in exchange." "What good is my birthright," Esau grunted,

"if I starve to death? Take it. It's yours!" That "trade" was a start, but there

was something else Jacob needed for all those promises to come to him—

his father's blessing. And, eventually, a chance came for that too. "Catch

something for me," Isaac said to Esau one day. He was old and **BLIND** and

had come to the end of his days. "Then bring it home and cook it up, just how

I LIKE IT. And after that I will give

you my BLESSING." Rebekah was listening.

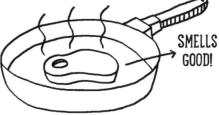

SMELLS GOOD!

And when she heard what Isaac wanted, she went and told Jacob.

"UH-OH!"

"Kill two goats!" she told him. "I'll cook them so they taste just like the meal that Esau will prepare. Then you can serve them to your father and receive the blessing instead!" "But he'll know it's me!" Jacob protested. "I'm not **HAIRY** like my brother." But Rebekah had a plan for that too! "We'll wrap your **NECK** and your **HANDS** in the skin of the goat," she said. "And if Isaac happens to touch you, he won't know the difference. Oh, and you'll 'borrow' some of Esau's CLOTHES as well, so you smell like him!" When Jacob entered his father's tent, roasted goat in goatskin-covered hand, he did his best to play "PRETEND ESAU." "Here's your food, Father!" he said. Isaac may have been blind, but he was no fool. "That was quick!" he replied. "And what's wrong with your **VOICE?** You sound remarkably like your brother, Jacob." Then he beckoned Jacob to come closer. He TOUCHED Jacob's "hairy" hand. He

"ESAU, IS THAT YOU?!"

SNIFFED at Jacob's "borrowed" clothing. And when he was

satisfied, he smiled and ate and said, "It is you, Esau! Here is my blessing!" YAY!

Jacob *HURRIED* back to Rebekah and the two of them **CELEBRATED**.

But when Esau returned some time later and took the meal he had prepared to

his father, he discovered what Jacob had done. And Jacob's celebration turned

 to **PANIC**. "Where is he?" Esau shouted. "Where is

my cheat of a brother? When I find him, I will kill him!"

So Jacob fled to Rebekah's homeland, **FEARING**

for his life. But Esau was not <u>done</u> with him. And neither

was **GOD**. For there was more, so much more to come...

A LADDER TO HEAVEN

RUNNING! Jacob was running. Running for his life. He had

CHEATED his twin brother, Esau, and stolen his inheritance.

So Esau was determined to kill him. "Go to my people!" his

mother, Rebekah, said. "Go to Haran and stay with my

brother **LABAN**. And find yourself a wife there." So

Jacob ran. And when he couldn't run anymore, his {breath} gone and

his legs cramping, Jacob fell down on the ground. He rested his **OUCH**

head on a big stone—not the comfiest PILLOW

choice—and fell into a deep, exhausted sleep. Then, suddenly, he

woke. Or at least it seemed as if he was awake, because his dream was so

real. A **LADDER** appeared before him—a ladder that reached **THAT'S A LONG WAY UP!**

from the dusty bit of (EARTH) where he lay right

into heaven. And the ladder was not empty.

No! On every step stood an angel,

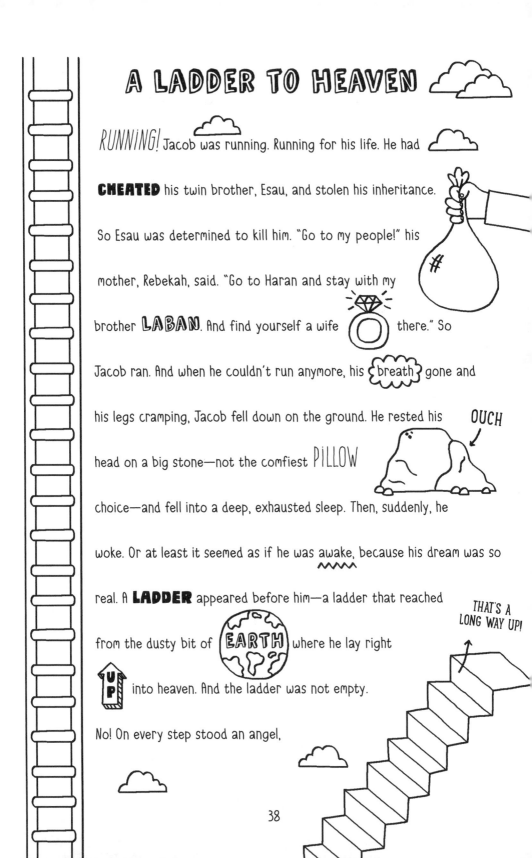

some stepping up and some stepping down—a flowing, GLOWING parade between heaven and earth.

On the final step, at the very top, stood **GOD** himself!

"I am the God of your grandfather Abraham," God announced, "and the God of your father Isaac too. The land on which you lie is my gift to you and to your **CHILDREN** and **GRANDCHILDREN** and all the children who follow. They will spread like dust—to the NORTH and the SOUTH and the EAST and the WEST. And through your family, I will bless every nation on earth! I will watch over you and PROTECT you and bring you, one day, back to this land. And I will not leave you until I have done everything I have promised." With that, the DREAM ended and Jacob OPENED his eyes.

"God is surely in this place!" he thought. "And I didn't even realize it!" When he did, he was **FRIGHTENED**, overcome with AWE and WONDER.

"This is nothing **LESS** than the house of God!" he cried. "And here is the gate of heaven!" So when morning came, Jacob took the stone on which he had rested his head and, setting it up on one end, turned his (PILLOW) into a pillar. Then he POURED oil on it, anointing it as a holy place—a place where God was. He called that place **BETHEL**, which means "the house of God." And he made this promise: "If God watches over me and provides **FOOD** for my belly and

THIS IS
THE HOUSE
OF GOD!

CLOTHES for my body and brings me back, in peace, to the land of my fathers, then he will be my God and this PILLAR will be his house!" Then off he went to his uncle Laban, dreams in his head and God's promise in his **HEART**. ♡

♡   ♡

ONE LONG, TRICKY ENGAGEMENT

When Jacob came to the homeland of his mother, Rebekah, all looked well. Quite LITERALLY, in fact, because there was a well. A BIG well. With three flocks of sheep gathered around it. The shepherds removed the stone covering the well so the sheep could drink. "Do you know a man called  Laban?" Jacob asked the shepherds. "He's my mother's brother." "Of course!" the SHEPHERDS replied. "Look, here comes his daughter, Rachel, with her sheep." Jacob looked. Rachel was BEAUTIFUL! And he

RACHEL

knew, right away, that she was the girl for him. He introduced himself.

He helped her water her sheep. Then Rachel took him to Laban. Jacob told Laban everything that had happened and **VOLUNTEERED** to work for him. "Nonsense," said Laban. "You're my relative. You can't work for free. You deserve to be paid!" "I'll take no money," Jacob said. "Instead,

let me marry your daughter Rachel." "Work 7 years," Laban said. "Then,

with my BLESSING, you can marry!" Jacob was delighted. And the seven long

years did not seem long to him at all as he got to

know Rachel and dreamed of the day they would be

MAN and WIFE. At last, that day came. The

THAT'S
NOT
RACHEL!

wedding passed, but when the bride was eventually revealed,

it wasn't Rachel whom Jacob had married, but her older sister, **LEAH**. "It's

what happens here," Laban grinned. "The older sister must be married first.

But if you work for me for another SEVEN YEARS..." he added. "You'll let

me marry Rachel?" Jacob asked. "With pleasure! In fact, give it a week and

you can marry her then. But you will still owe me seven years of labor!"

Jacob had been tricked. And it was probably the least that a

trickster like him deserved. But he **LOVED** Rachel. So he agreed. Leah gave

birth to lots of children but, for a long time, Rachel had none. Then, finally, she gave Jacob a son. A little boy called **JOSEPH**. It was her dream come true. And Jacob's too. Dreaming would play a BIG part in Joseph's

story as well. Before that, though, Jacob needed to return to his

homeland. God told him to, and **PROMISED** to be with him if he did. But

Jacob hadn't seen his brother Esau for many years, and he was afraid that

Esau would still want to kill him. So he sent a huge menagerie of **GOATS**,

SHEEP, CAMELS, and **DONKEYS** ahead of him as a gift for Esau.

Then he prayed to God and asked for his protection, reminding God of the

promise he had made. That night, someone came to Jacob and wrestled with

him. That someone injured Jacob's hip, but Jacob would not let go. "Bless

me!" Jacob said, "and I will release you." "Your name is

Jacob," the someone said. "But from now on you will be

ROUND 1

called **ISRAEL**, a name that means 'you have WRESTLED with God!'"

Then God blessed Jacob and Jacob limped away. When he

came to his homeland and Esau was in sight, Jacob walked

ahead of his FAMILY and all the animals he had accumulated to go meet him. Jacob was a very RICH man now. And so was Esau! When he came to Jacob, he embraced him and forgave him. The twins were BROTHERS again! Ah, but families grow and this one did too. It wasn't perfect. What family is? Life wasn't PERFECT, either. But God had made a promise, a PROMISE to bless the world through that family. So he did, even when things weren't perfect. For there was more, so much more to come…

THIS WAY FOR MORE STORIES!

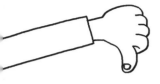
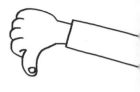

NOT-SO-HAPPY FAMILIES

You'd **THINK** Jacob would have learned. He had been his mother Rebekah's **FAVORITE**. And Jacob's father, Isaac, had favored his brother, Esau. It caused trouble between them for years. So you'd think Jacob would have tried to love his **12** sons equally. **NOPE**. His second-youngest son, Joseph, was the child of Rachel, the wife he truly loved. And as she had died giving birth to the youngest boy, **BENJAMIN**, those two received most of his AFFECTION. Benjamin was still a baby, but Joseph was old enough to have his father's full attention. And that displayed itself (quite literally!) in the shape of a **BEAUTIFUL** multicolored coat. It was brilliant! It was

PRETTY FANCY COAT!

bright! It was flowing! It was nice! It was the fanciest coat for **MILES** around. Joseph's brothers had nothing like it. But it wasn't just the coat that got their goat. No, it was the way Joseph treated them. He would snitch on them when they did things they shouldn't. And Jacob always believed Joseph. ALWAYS! Then there were the **DREAMS**. Joseph was 17 or so when they started. And they were so annoying! "I had a dream!" he announced to his brothers one day, his robe flowing around him. "We were tying up sheaves of wheat in a field. And you'll never guess what happened. My sheaf stood UP straight and yours all bowed down before it!" "What are you saying?" his brothers SHOUTED. "That you'll rule over us someday?" And they hated Joseph even more. A few days later, Joseph announced, "I've had another dream!" His robe shone brightly —in the midday light. "This time, the SUN, the MOON, and eleven STARS all bowed down before me!" When Jacob heard it, even he was annoyed. "Are you suggesting that your brothers and your mother and I will bow before you too?"

Jacob never forgot that dream. Neither did Joseph's brothers. But while it made old Jacob wonder about its meaning, it made Joseph's brothers **HATE** him more than ever. So, one day, when Jacob sent Joseph out into the **PASTURES** to see how the brothers were doing,  they came up with a plan. "Here comes the dreamer," they grumbled. "Let's kill him and throw his body into a pit. We'll see what becomes of his dreams then!" But one of the brothers, REUBEN, wasn't so happy with this plan. "We don't need to kill him!" he said. "Why don't we just throw him into the pit and **SCARE** him?" When Joseph arrived, they grabbed him, tore off his beautiful coat, and threw him into the pit.

Reuben left, hoping to go back and RESCUE Joseph when his brothers had

gone. But in the meantime, a caravan of ISHMAELITE traders

wandered by. "Why kill our brother," asked Judah, "when we can sell him

as a slave to these traders? We'll still be rid of him and we'll make a tidy

PROFIT as well!" So that's what they did. They sold

Joseph for twenty pieces of silver. When Reuben returned and learned what

they had done, he was **HORRIFIED**. Still, they had to

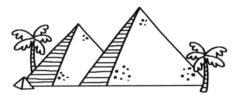

IT WASN'T ME! tell their father something. So they

smeared Joseph's beautiful coat with the blood

of a goat and took it to Jacob. "He was TORN to

pieces by a wild animal," they lied, while Jacob cried and cried. "I will mourn

my boy until I die," he wept. And Joseph? Joseph the DREAMER was carried

away and sold as a slave in Egypt.

But God remembered his promise.

Of course he did! So there was more, so much more to come...

JOSEPH'S TIME IN JAIL

The Ishmaelites sold Joseph to one of **PHARAOH'S** officers, a man called

POTIPHAR, who was captain of the guard. It looked as though Joseph's

dreams would amount to . But it was God who had put those

dreams in his head. And it was God who helped Joseph, even though he was a

 slave. So God made sure that all went well for Joseph and his new

master: Potiphar's fields YIELDED more food; his household was

HAPPIER; all that Joseph touched was blessed with SUCCESS. And it wasn't

long before Potiphar put Joseph in charge of all he had! But Joseph was

handsome. A good-looking, fit young man. And Potiphar's wife

REALLY LIKED him. She wanted to kiss Joseph—and spend time with

him. But Joseph would have none of it. "I will not **BETRAY** my master or

 sin against my God!" he told her. She wouldn't

give up, though, and one day when she was

alone in the house with Joseph, she tried to **GRAB** hold

of him. He ran from her and all she got hold of was the coat he was wearing (not

multicolored this time, but a problem **NONETHELESS**). Angry

that Joseph had rejected her, she held the coat up in front

of the other servants when they returned. "Joseph tried to LIE!

KISS me and I **FOUGHT** him off. Here is his coat as

proof!" Worse still, when Potiphar came home, she told

him the same lie. Potiphar believed her and Joseph

was sent to PRISON. Again, it looked as if Joseph's

 dreams had come to nothing. But, once more, God was there to help him.

Everything Joseph touched in that prison was blessed with **SUCCESS**,

until at last he was put in charge of all the prisoners! One day, Pharaoh was very

angry with his chief CUPBEARER and his chief BAKER. Who knows

why? The odd wine **SPILL?** The occasional bit of **BURNT**

THIS TOAST HAS SEEN BUTTER DAYS!

toast? When they arrived at the prison, Joseph was charged with taking care of

them. And that's when the **DREAMS** began. Not Joseph's dreams but the dreams of the **CUPBEARER** and the **BAKER**. When Joseph went

to attend to them one morning, both men looked sad and confused.

"We each had dreams last night," they said, TREMBLING. "And we don't know what

they mean!" "Tell me your dreams," whispered

Joseph, "and God will show me what they mean." "In

my dream," said the cupbearer, "there was a **GRAPEVINE**

with 3 branches. I SQUEEZED the grapes into Pharaoh's

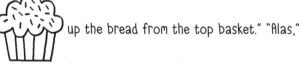

cup and gave it to him." "The meaning is clear," said Joseph. "In three days'

time, you will be set FREE and will once again be Pharaoh's

cupbearer!" Encouraged, the baker told Joseph his dream. "There were 3

baskets of **BREAD** balanced on my head. And the birds came and gobbled

up the bread from the top basket." "Alas,"

said Joseph sadly, "in three days, Pharaoh will put

you to death and leave you for the birds to

eat." **BOTH** dreams came **TRUE**,

52

the **HAPPY** one and the **SAD** one. But even though the cupbearer

PROMISED to remember Joseph and do something to him, he

forgot. **FORGOT** for  years, in fact, until Pharaoh himself had

some troubling dreams...

PHARAOH'S WACKY DREAMS

Pharaoh's dream went something like this. He (YUMMY!) was standing on the banks of the (Nile River), when **7 FAT**, healthy cows waded up out of the water and started to feed on the reedy grass. Behind them came **7** SCRAWNY, SCRAGGLY cows. But instead of eating the grass, the scrawny cows **GOBBLED** up the fat ones. It was not a nice dream—cows chewing on cows—and Pharaoh woke with a start. But just as he managed to fall back to sleep, Pharaoh had a second dream. This time, he was out in the fields when he saw seven fat, healthy heads of grain growing on one tall stalk. And, yes, behind them grew seven SCRAWNY, SCRAGGLY heads of grain, **TORN**

by the east wind. As Pharaoh watched, the

seven scrawny heads of grain grew mouths, somehow, and gobbled 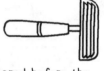 the

healthy, fat ones. This was even more disturbing, so, when morning came,

Pharaoh SUMMONED every sorcerer and sage in Egypt to tell him

what the dreams meant. Not one of them could do it. That's

when Pharaoh's cupbearer FINALLY remembered Joseph! "There

was a man with me in prison," the cupbearer said. "He told me the meaning of

my dream. And he was right. Perhaps he can tell you the **MEANING** of yours."

Pharaoh sent for Joseph. And when Joseph had been shaved

 and dressed in a clean set of clothes, he appeared before the

ruler of all Egypt! "I understand you interpret dreams," said Pharaoh. "*I don't,*"

Joseph replied, "but the **LORD GOD** does and he will tell me what your

dreams mean." So Pharaoh told Joseph his dreams. And God told Joseph what

they meant. "The DREAMS are the same," Joseph explained. "For **SEVEN**

years, your crops will grow and your land will prosper. But those

SEVEN years will be followed by **SEVEN** years of famine, when nothing will grow. The fact that there were two dreams means this

will happen right away and you need to act **QUICKLY**.

Put someone in charge of STORING up food these next

seven years so you will still have enough to **EAT** when the famine comes."

Pharaoh smiled. "What **BETTER** person than you?" he said. "The man whose

God showed me the meaning of my dreams. You will ORGANIZE

this for us. My people will do whatever you tell them. And

only I, who sit on the throne, will be more **POWERFUL**

than you." So, just like that, Joseph went from

prison to the second-HIGHEST position in all of Egypt! He was given

Pharaoh's SIGNET RING. A gold chain was hung around his

neck. And he was dressed in a very nice coat (**ONCE AGAIN!**).

Joseph was **30** years old by this time. And just as God

had done in Potiphar's house and in the prison, he helped Joseph.

PRETTY
BIG RING!

And everything Joseph did was blessed with success. Grain was **STORED**, and when the famine came, there was **PLENTY** for everyone to eat. Even

foreigners who came SEEKING food. Foreigners, like **10** hungry

brothers from the land of **CANAAN**...

THE GOLDEN CUP TEST

The **FAMINE** had spread to the land of Canaan, so when **JACOB** heard

 there was food in Egypt, he sent his sons to buy what they could.

"Go, the **10** of you," he said. "**BENJAMIN** will stay here

with me." Jacob was afraid that HARM would come to his youngest son, just

as it had to his brother, Joseph. So off the other brothers went. When they

WHO'S THIS GUY?!

 were led to Joseph to buy food, they didn't

LET'S TEST THEM! recognize him. Ten years and more had passed.

He looked just like an Egyptian. He SPOKE the language

of an Egyptian too. But Joseph recognized his brothers at once. He didn't

TRUST them, though. He hadn't forgotten what they'd done to him. So he

put them to the TEST. "Tell them they are spies," he said to his interpreter,

 "who have come to find our weaknesses!" "No!" they cried.

"We are simply **12** hungry brothers from Canaan. Well,

ten, as you see. The YOUNGEST is at home with our father.

And our other brother is…no more." That **REMINDER** did not please

Joseph. "To prove you are NOT spies," he said, "bring me your YOUNGEST

brother. One of you will stay with me until you do." Then he put all of them

in jail for **3** days. When they were brought before Joseph

again, Reuben grunted to his brothers in their HEBREW

language, "I knew something like this would happen! We are all

guilty. This is **PUNISHMENT** for what we did to our brother!" They

SNEAKY!

thought no one could understand, but, of course, Joseph could. He turned

and wept at the MEMORY of what they'd done. Then he

sent them away, keeping Simeon until they returned. And he

ORDERED his servants to fill their sacks not only with

grain but also with the MONEY they had paid him! When the brothers got

home to Canaan, they told their father what Joseph had

said. "No!" Jacob replied. "I've already LOST one son.

I will not lose another!" Then they found the money with

YOUNG JOSEPH

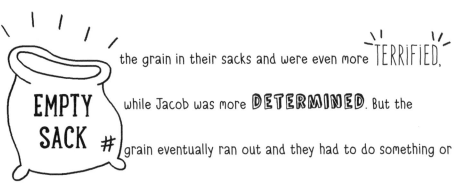

the grain in their sacks and were even more TERRIFIED,

while Jacob was more **DETERMINED**. But the

grain eventually ran out and they had to do something or

STARVE. So Jacob gave in and Benjamin went to Egypt with his brothers to

buy more food. When he saw Benjamin, Joseph INVITED them all to his

HOUSE. The brothers were afraid he was going to **PUNISH**

them because of the money in their sacks, so they apologized. But Joseph

told them not to worry. He served them a meal and asked about their father,

and they were AMAZED. When the time came to send them

on their way, Joseph gave them one final test. "Hide one of

my **GOLD CUPS** in the youngest brother's sack," he

ordered his servants. Then, as they left the city, Joseph had them

arrested again! **"THIEVES!"** he shouted. "Your youngest

NICE CUP!

brother will stay here as my slave!" "No, please!" they BEGGED. "This will kill

our father." "Keep me, instead," said Judah, the very brother who had sold

Joseph to the **ISHMAELITES**. It was SURPRISE!

at that moment Joseph knew his brothers had changed.

Weeping, he sent his servants from the room.

Then he said, "It's me. Your brother. Joseph." The brothers were both

TERRIFIED and AMAZED. "Don't worry," Joseph assured them. "You meant

to hurt me, I know. But **GOD** has used that to **SAVE** our

GO!

family and provide a place where we can prosper. Go, fetch our

father and bring him here. It's time for us to be TOGETHER again!" And

in a way no one expected, pretty much everyone's dream

came true.

BUT THAT'S NOT THE END OF THE STORY!

THE BABY WHO SAILED THE NILE

Joseph and his brothers THRIVED in Egypt. They had **CHILDREN** and their

CHILDREN had **CHILDREN**, and their **CHILDREN** after them. God's

promise to Abraham was definitely coming **TRUE**. The children of Israel, or

the Hebrews as they came to be called, were becoming a very **BIG**

family indeed! HUNDREDS of years passed. Then a pharaoh came to the

throne of Egypt who no longer remembered Joseph and what he had done

to save the Egyptian people. All that pharaoh saw were Hebrews. Hebrews

everywhere! And that **FRIGHTENED** him. "They are not Egyptians. They

are different! What if they join with our enemies and fight

against us?" he said. So Pharaoh made the Hebrews his SLAVES. He put

taskmasters over them, who treated them

harshly. They worked Pharaoh's fields

and they built Pharaoh's buildings—great cities full of

them, called **PITHOM** and **RAMESES**. And as if that wasn't bad enough,

he told the Egyptian **MIDWIVES** to kill all Hebrew baby boys the second

they were BORN! Fortunately, the midwives disobeyed him. "We try,"

they told him. "But those Hebrew women are so **STRONG**, they have

their babies even before we get there!" God blessed those midwives. And he

went on blessing his people, the Hebrews, too. So Pharaoh came up with an

even more devious plan. "If you see a Hebrew baby boy," he ordered ALL his

people, "throw him in the Nile River!"

SOMETHING SIMILAR HAPPENS AT THE BIRTH OF ANOTHER VERY IMPORTANT BABY IN THE NEW TESTAMENT...

DO YOU KNOW WHO THIS IS?

Now, there was a Hebrew woman, descended from Joseph's brother LEVI, who

was **DETERMINED** that her child would not die . So when she gave

birth to her son, she did her best to hide him. But babies big.

63

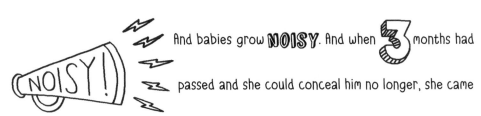

And babies grow **NOISY**. And when **3** months had passed and she could conceal him no longer, she came up with a clever plan. She built him a little basket boat made out of bulrushes.

She covered it with STICKY tar and pitch so it would not soak up **WATER** and sink. Then she put her **BOY** in the basket and set it floating among the reeds on the banks of the **NILE RIVER**.

Plus, she sent her daughter to hide on the bank and keep watch over the basket and the boy. It seemed like a PERFECT plan. That is, until Pharaoh's daughter decided to bathe in the river. She **SPOTTED**

LOOK, A BABY! the basket and sent her serving girls to fetch it. And when she opened it, what a...

Trembling, the boy's sister watched **HELPLESSLY**, waiting for the moment her brother would be flung into the Nile. But no. One **SURPRISE** followed another. The baby began to cry and Pharaoh's daughter felt sorry for him. "It's a Hebrew child," she said gently. And she **HELD** him. And she **CUDDLED** him. The sister saw her chance and popped up from the reeds. "I know a Hebrew woman who could nurse him for you!" she said. "Fetch her, girl!" Pharaoh's daughter commanded.

The girl returned with her mom. "Nurse this child for me," said Pharaoh's daughter. "I will pay you for your trouble. And when he no *LONGER* needs your milk, bring him back to me and I will bring him up as my son. And seeing as I pulled him up out of the water, that is what I will call him. Little 'pulled up.'

Little **MOSES**."

WHAT WILL HAPPEN NEXT?

THE CHATTY BURNING BUSH

WHOA!

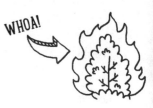

 grew up in the house of Pharaoh's daughter, but he NEVER

forgot who he really was or who his suffering, enslaved people were. One day,

he saw an Egyptian BEATING a Hebrew. Moses looked around to check no

one was watching. Then he struck the Egyptian

down dead and buried his body in the sand.

The next day, he saw two Hebrews FIGHTING

with each other. "Why are you doing that?" he asked.

 KILL HIM! "Who made you boss?" answered one of the men.

"Are you going to kill us like you killed that Egyptian?" The

word was out! Moses was TERRIFIED. And before long,

Pharaoh gave the (command) that Moses should die. So

Moses ran. Ran from his adopted country and his own people. Ran to the

land of MIDIAN. And that's where Moses made his home. He saved a

woman called **ZIPPORAH** and her **6** sisters from a gang of nasty

shepherds. He married her. They had a son. And for years and

years, Moses tended the flocks of his father-in-law, JETHRO.

Then, one day, while he and his sheep were minding their own business on the

grassy slopes of a mountain called **HOREB**, Moses saw a bush burst into

FLAMES. Whoosh! The fire burned hot and the fire burned BRIGHT, but it

didn't burn up the bush. Strange! So Moses crept closer for a better

look. That's when a voice crackled out from the not-quite-

burning branches. "Moses!" the voice called. "I'm here!" the

stunned shepherd replied. "Take a step back and slip off your sandals," said

the voice. "For I am the **GOD** of your fathers. The God of ABRAHAM, ISAAC,

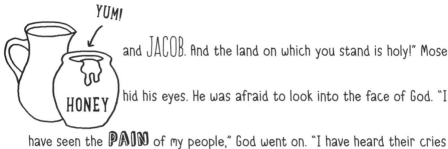
YUM!

and JACOB. And the land on which you stand is holy!" Moses hid his eyes. He was afraid to look into the face of God. "I have seen the PAIN of my people," God went on. "I have heard their cries for help. I know they're suffering. So I've come to rescue them and take them to a home of their own. A land flowing with MILK and HONEY! And I want you, Moses, to go to Pharaoh and tell him to set my people FREE!" "But I'm a nobody!" cried Moses. "Why me?" "One day, you and all your people  will WORSHIP me on this very mountain," said God. "And then you will know why I've chosen you." "And if they ask who sent me," Moses replied. "What name shall I give?" "Tell them I AM sent you," God replied. "The God of their fathers." "But what if they don't believe me?" asked Moses. "Throw your staff on the ground," God said. Moses did and it turned into a SNAKE! "Now pick it up again," said God. And it turned back into a staff. "Show them that and they'll believe you!" Moses still wasn't convinced. "Put your hand INSIDE your cloak," God said.

CAN YOU NAME ANY MORE MIRACLES FOUND IN THE BIBLE? HINT: JESUS DID QUITE A FEW...

☆ MIRACLES ☆

"Then pull it out again." When Moses did, his hand was covered with a disease.

"Now do the same again," God said. And when Moses did, his hand was healed!

But Moses still DOUBTED. So God told him that, when he stood

before Pharaoh, he should POUR water from the **NILE** River

onto the ground. "It will turn to blood," God promised him. "I'm no good at

speaking!" Moses stammered. "I won't know what to say." "I made your mouth,"

God persisted. "I will give you the WORDS. And if you're still worried, take

your brother **AARON** with you, to speak on your behalf." So, every excuse

dismissed, the old shepherd left his sheep and went with his brother to face

 Pharaoh, the ruler of Egypt.

PHARAOH'S FIASCO OF FROGS AND FLIES

When **MOSES** and **AARON** went to see Pharaoh, they spoke to him plainly.

"The God of the Hebrews has sent us," they said. "He wants you to let his people go so they can WORSHIP him in the wilderness." Then

NOT AGAIN!

they did the "staff into serpent" TRICK to show that they meant business. Pharaoh smiled and calmly sent for his own

MAGICIANS. And they did exactly the same TRICK! "Set the Hebrews free?" Pharaoh shrugged his shoulders. "I don't think so." So Moses and Aaron went back the next day. They touched the staff to the Nile River and it turned to BLOOD. The fish died. The water

URGH!

was undrinkable. It was disgusting. Again, Pharaoh called for his magicians. Again, they did exactly the SAME thing. And, again, he shrugged and said, "My Hebrew slaves are staying put!" Seven days passed. And when Moses and Aaron went back,

they had just one word for Pharaoh: "**FROGS**."

When Aaron STRETCHED his staff over the Nile, out

they came, HOPPING everywhere. Into **OVENS** and onto

HEADS and even into the **BOWLS** where the Egyptians made

their bread. Turns out that Pharaoh's **MAGICIANS** could do

the frog thing too, but Pharaoh had had enough. "Go on, then," he sighed.

"Take your people into the wilderness." So the frogs all died and, oh dear, the

smell! But when the frogs were no longer a problem for him, Pharaoh changed

his mind. "The Hebrews will stay!" he said. So God sent swarms of flies,

BUZZING into the Egyptians' houses and food and eyes. But he built a

 kind of **INVISIBLE** wall between them and his own people

and not one Hebrew family was troubled.

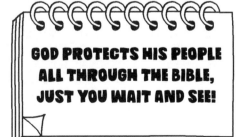

GOD PROTECTS HIS PEOPLE
ALL THROUGH THE BIBLE,
JUST YOU WAIT AND SEE!

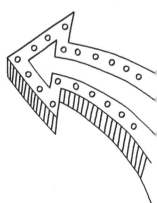

"Your people can go!" Pharaoh cried to Moses and Aaron. "Just **PHEW!** make these flies **FLY** away!" But, again, at the last minute, his heart grew hard and he changed his mind. So God killed the Egyptian CAMELS and HORSES, DONKEYS and GOATS and SHEEP. But the animals that belonged to the Hebrews all survived. Pharaoh didn't even blink. His heart was well and **TRULY** hard by now. "You're going nowhere," he grunted.

He did the same when his people were covered in BOILS, and when his crops were knocked down by **HAIL**, and when what food remained was eaten by **LOCUSTS**, and when DARKNESS covered the land for 3 whole days. "I have one more plague to send," God told Moses. "And I believe that this one will FINALLY make the difference. I am going to **STRIKE** down dead the firstborn child of **EVERY** Egyptian and the firstborn offspring of every Egyptian animal. So there are some things

my people need to do if they are to survive this.

Every family must kill a lamb and spread its blood

on the DOORPOST of their house and on the

LINTEL above the door too. Then they must cook the

lamb and eat it with bitter herbs and bread without yeast. And they must

eat it in a HURRY, with their sandals on and their belts

fastened and their staffs in their hands, as if they are about to

leave on a long journey. And at **MIDNIGHT**, I will bring **DEATH** to the

Egyptian firstborn. But I will pass over the houses where I see the blood of

the lamb." Everything happened just as God said. The Egyptian firstborn died.

The Hebrew firstborn lived. And, FINALLY, his hard heart now

broken by the death of his **OWN** son,

Pharaoh let the Hebrew people go.

THE (SALTY) TASTE OF FREEDOM

Pharaoh wasn't the only one who wanted the Hebrews to leave. ORDINARY

Egyptians did too, because they had also lost their firstborn children. "Go! Before

we all die!" they cried. So out of Egypt the Hebrews went, **SIX HUNDRED**

THOUSAND of them! And because there was not even time for the bread

 they were making to **RISE**, they left it unleavened—that is, without

yeast—in the bowls that they bundled up and carried with them.

And so God gave Moses ways for the Hebrews to {remember} what he

had done for them. "From this time on," he told Moses, "my people

must CELEBRATE a feast of unleavened bread, to remember what happened

when I set them **FREE**. They must also celebrate the PASSOVER, to

REMEMBER how I passed over their houses and struck the Egyptians dead.

And because their FREEDOM was won by the

 I BELONG TO GOD!

death of the firstborn children of the Egyptians, they

must **DEDICATE** their firstborn children, and their firstborn animals, to me."

Then God led that **GREAT** multitude toward the Red Sea. Led them by

a pillar of **CLOUD** in the day and a pillar of **FIRE** by night!

But as the Hebrews journeyed, celebrating their newfound

freedom, Pharaoh **CHANGED** his mind. "Why should I let

my slaves go?" he growled. Then he climbed into his chariot and, accompanied

by six hundred more chariots, he *CHASED* after the Hebrews. When the

Hebrews saw the Red Sea before them and the chariots **CHARGING** up

behind them, they cried out to Moses, "Have you brought us this far just

to let us die? We would have been better off slaving away in Egypt than

dying out here in this desert!" "Don't be afraid," Moses told them. "Stay calm

and **TRUST** the Lord. He will fight for you!" And so

God did. The pillar of cloud moved between

the chariots and the Hebrews, covering

and confusing the Egyptians. Then God told Moses to **RAISE** his staff

and stretch out his hand. And when he did, the sea PARTED! A wall of water

stood tall on one side and a wall stood tall on the other side as well. And

down through the middle, God made a **PATH** for his people. Along that path

they walked, all **600,000** of them. The Egyptians

came after them, of course. But the pillars of cloud and fire confused

them. And the muddy floor clogged their chariot wheels and slowed

them to a CRAWL. And, finally, when Moses and the people

had safely crossed to the other side, Moses stretched his

hand out over the sea again, and the water walls **TUMBLED** in waves over

the chariots, and Pharaoh and his army all drowned. Free, finally and truly

FREE , the Hebrews **DANCED** and **CELEBRATED**. Moses

and Aaron's sister Miriam picked up a tambourine and led the women in a

song:

**SING TO GOD.
CELEBRATE HIS AMAZING
VICTORY. FOR HE HAS
THROWN THE HORSE
AND ITS RIDER DEEP
DOWN INTO THE SEA!**

SING ALONG!

INTO THE WILDERNESS

The Hebrews were free at last! Free to cross the **WILDERNESS** to a home they could call their own. They should have been **HAPPY**, but they **GRUMBLED**. "We're hungry, Moses! Did you bring us out here to starve?" So Moses went to God. And God sent **QUAIL** for the people to EAT in the evening, and something called manna—bread from **HEAVEN**—for them to eat when the morning dew had lifted. The people liked the quail and the manna, but they STILL grumbled. "We need water, Moses! Did you bring us out here so we would die of thirst?" So Moses went to God. And God gave the people water—from out of a **ROCK!** Then God called Moses to the top of MOUNT SINAI. There, he gave Moses the rules he wanted his people to live by. Rules about **HONORING** God and treating each other well, and **CARING** for foreigners and the poor. There were

YUM!

QUITE A CLIMB!

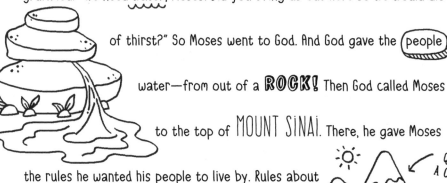

TEN COMMANDMENTS and more, all meant to show, to the Hebrews and the WHOLE WORLD, what a life lived God's way would look like. God wrote them on two **TABLETS** of stone. He also gave Moses instructions for building the tabernacle—a tent where the people could **WORSHIP** him.

Moses was on the mountain for so long, however, that the people began to GRUMBLE again. And because he was gone, they grumbled to AARON instead. "Where is Moses? Is he ever coming back or is he just going to leave us here?" Then they melted down their jewelry and made a **GOLDEN** idol shaped like a calf, which they

PRAISE THE COW!

worshiped as their god! God was not happy. He had just shown his people how much he loved them by rescuing them from **SLAVERY**. Now they were worshiping a man-made god who couldn't do anything! "I will destroy these **UNFAITHFUL** people and make a new nation from your

children instead," God told Moses. But Moses **BEGGED** God to remember the

promises he had made to ABRAHAM, ISAAC, and JACOB, to make their family

a blessing to the world. So God **SPARED** his people. On and on they

journeyed, getting EVER closer to the land God had **PROMISED** their

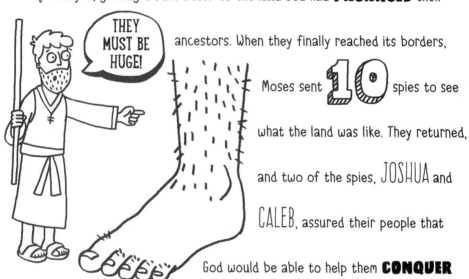

ancestors. When they finally reached its borders,

Moses sent 10 spies to see

what the land was like. They returned,

and two of the spies, JOSHUA and

CALEB, assured their people that

God would be able to help them **CONQUER**

the land. But the other eight were terrified. "The people are like GIANTS!"

they cried. "Their cities are **SURROUNDED** by walls so TALL we will

never knock them down." Once again, the people grumbled. "Have you

brought us all this way to be killed by giants?" Finally, God was fed up.

"Apart from Joshua and Caleb," he declared, "not one of you will survive to enter the land I have promised you. For **40** long years, you will wander in the **WILDERNESS**. Then and only then will you find your way in." And so it was. For forty years, the Hebrews wandered and waited. ← THAT'S A LONG TIME TO WAIT!

WOW!

Even Moses died, but not before **GOD** had taken him to a MOUNTAINTOP to let him see the land. Then, when a new generation was in place, God parted the waters of the **JORDAN RIVER**, just as he'd parted the Red Sea. And into the promised land they went. And, yes, there was **MORE**, so much **MORE** to come. For the BIG family God had rescued needed to conquer the land. More than that, they needed to learn how to live there in a way that pleased God and would honor him as their king.

81

THE BATTLE OF JERICHO

THERE ARE SO MANY!
↓

There was nothing about the INSTRUCTIONS that was normal. But then

Joshua had grown used to worshiping a God who specialized in "not normal!"

TEN plagues, a **SEA** parted. A **RIVER** too, for that matter.

BREAD from heaven, **WATER** from rocks. The list went on

and on. So when the angel appeared—the

MIRACLE CHECKLIST
☐ _____
☐ _____
☐ _____
☐ _____
☐ _____

commander of the Lord's own army—and told Joshua

God's plan for conquering Jericho, Joshua just nodded.

Given what God had already done for his people, this seemed

PERFECTLY normal! Spies had already been sent into the city, before

the Hebrews had even crossed the Jordan River. And although the king of

Jericho had **DISCOVERED** them, the spies had escaped. "A woman

called Rahab hid us," they explained. "Then she lowered us with a

rope through her window and down the outside wall to safety. We

have **PROMISED** to spare her and her whole family when

we conquer the city. She will tie a red **RIBBON** to her window so we know where she is." Joshua smiled.

Red on the <u>doorposts</u> had saved EVERY Hebrew firstborn back in Egypt. And if they managed to

PRETTY FANCY!

conquer the city, **RED** would save this woman, Rahab, as well. More of

God's normal! The plan was, in many ways, quite simple.

The ark of the covenant was at the HEART of it.

It was a special box, kept in the tabernacle. It

contained the tablets of stone Moses had carried down from the mountain—

the tablets that told them God's law. Aaron's **STAFF** was in there too—

the one he had used to do battle with the Egyptian magicians. And, FINALLY,

there was a jar of manna. It was a sign of God's presence—

his **LAW**, his **POWER**, and his **PROVISION**. The plan was to carry the

ark in a kind of parade around the walls of the city. Walking before the ark

would be 7 priests blowing seven TRUMPETS. And in front of them and behind them, the soldiers would march. No one

one was to SHOUT or {SCREAM} or even speak.

The only sound would be the blowing of the trumpets.

Not the **NORMAL** way to conquer a city. Not by a long shot!

So Joshua gave God's plan to his army and, strange as those instructions

must have seemed to the men, that's exactly what they did. For **6** days,

they marched around the wall. Marched around just once. Trumpets blowing.

Soldiers silent. Then, on the seventh day, they marched around the city

again. Trumpets blowing. Soldiers silent. But on this day, they marched

around another time. Then a **THIRD** time, and then a **FOURTH** and

FIFTH and **SIXTH** time. When they marched around for the seventh time,

something different happened.

THAT'S A LOT OF WALKING!

"SHOUT!" cried Joshua to his army. "Raise your voices as loud as you can, for God has given you this city!" And when they did, their shouts were **ECHOED** by another sound—the sharp **CRACKING** of mortar and **SPLITTING** of stones. The GREAT wall of Jericho came falling down! The city was conquered. Rahab's family was spared. Just another ORDINARY, EVERYDAY, NORMAL victory, by a God who was anything but normal!

I'M CRACKING UP!

A WOMAN'S VICTORY

After Joshua died, God appointed people called judges to lead Israel. One part of their job was to sort out **PROBLEMS** between people, like JUDGES do today. But they were also in charge of gathering armies and defending the country when the people of Israel were **ATTACKED** by their enemies. These attacks usually happened when the people forgot about God and worshiped other gods. And that was exactly the situation when **JABIN**, the king of Canaan, came to crush the people of Israel. For long years, he oppressed them with his army and his nine hundred chariots of iron! Finally, as often happened, the people turned back in desperation to God and cried out for his And, on this occasion, God appointed a prophet called DEBORAH to be their judge and to rescue them. She sent for a man called **BARAK** and gave him this message from God: "Gather an army of ten thousand men at **TABOR** Mountain. Then

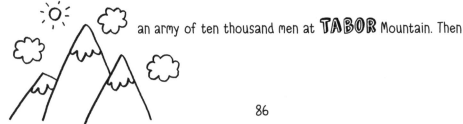

go and fight Jabin's general, **SISERA**, at the Kishon River and I will give you the victory!" Barak _thought_ about this for a moment and then gave his answer. "I will do it," he said to Deborah, "if, and only if, you come with me." Deborah GRINNED. She was listening to God again. "I will go with you," she replied. "But if I do, the glory of this victory will not be yours. No. God will use a woman to defeat Sisera, and he says that the glory will be hers!" So Sisera gathered his 900 chariots at the Kishon River. Barak and his ten thousand men stormed down from Tabor Mountain. And, amid the clashing of **SWORDS** and the CRASHING of chariot **WHEELS**, the outcome Deborah prophesied came to pass: Sisera and his army were defeated! RUNNING for his life, Sisera found a place to hide in the tent of a woman called **JAEL**. "Come inside. Come and hide," she said to the general. "There's nothing here to fear." So into the TENT Sisera

COZY!

went and Jael covered him with a rug.

GIRL POWER!

87

"I'm so **THIRSTY**," he said. "Could you give me something to drink?" "Of course," Jael replied. "Here, have some milk." Sisera drank the milk GRATEFULLY and, when he had finished, he yawned. "I am so **TIRED**. I need to sleep. Would you GUARD the door of the tent? And if anyone comes looking for me, would you tell them that I am not here?" "Of course," said Jael again. But she had other plans. This was the man who had commanded 900 chariots; the general of Jabin's army who had cruelly CRUSHED the land. So, as soon as he was in a deep sleep, she took a HAMMER and drove a tent **PEG** through his head. OUCH! And when Barak came

HE'S IN THERE!

looking for him, she drew aside the tent flap and said, "Here is the man you seek." As Barak looked at the body of the **DEAD** general, he REMEMBERED Deborah's words: "God will use a WOMAN to defeat Sisera."

GOD HAS USED MANY OTHER WOMEN TO FULFILL HIS PURPOSES! TURN TO PAGE 148 TO READ ABOUT AN EXTRA SPECIAL WOMAN . . .

And so it was that Israel was rescued. Until, of course, they worshiped other gods AGAIN and fell into the hands of their enemies, and God had to raise up ANOTHER judge, and ANOTHER judge, and ANOTHER judge to save them. And, no, God hadn't forgotten his promise—that BIG promise to use Abraham's family to bring a  child into the WORLD. He was always working on that, even if he sometimes needed to use someone from a different family . . .

FAMILY LOYALTY

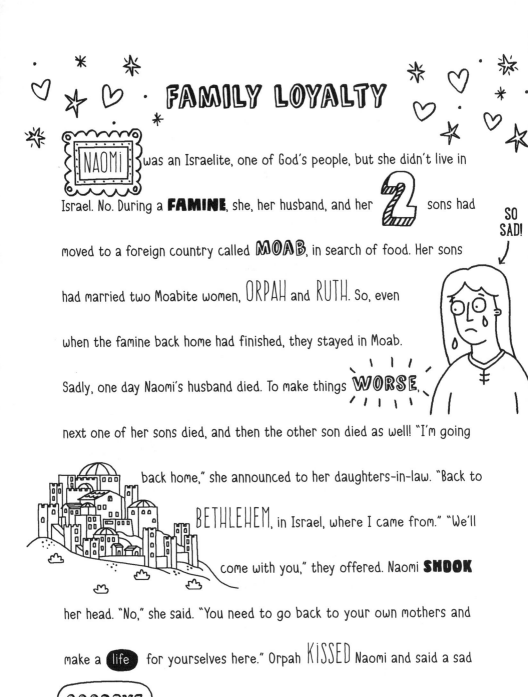

NAOMI was an Israelite, one of God's people, but she didn't live in Israel. No. During a **FAMINE**, she, her husband, and her **2** sons had moved to a foreign country called **MOAB**, in search of food. Her sons had married two Moabite women, ORPAH and RUTH. So, even when the famine back home had finished, they stayed in Moab. Sadly, one day Naomi's husband died. To make things **WORSE**, next one of her sons died, and then the other son died as well! "I'm going back home," she announced to her daughters-in-law. "Back to BETHLEHEM, in Israel, where I came from." "We'll come with you," they offered. Naomi **SHOOK** her head. "No," she said. "You need to go back to your own mothers and make a life for yourselves here." Orpah KISSED Naomi and said a sad **GOODBYE**.

SO SAD!

But Ruth wouldn't leave her mother-in-law. "I'm going with you," she insisted.

"Your **PEOPLE** will be my **PEOPLE** and your **GOD** will be my **GOD**." So

off they went. And they arrived in Bethlehem just in time for the barley harvest.

BOAZ, a relative of Naomi's dead husband, owned lots of fields, and Naomi

sent Ruth to pick up the bits of barley the harvesters had left behind.

This was a custom called **GLEANING**, which made sure the **POOR** had

something to eat. It was part of the law God had given to his PEOPLE. Boaz

had heard what Ruth had done for Naomi. He told his workers to make sure she

gathered as much **GRAIN** as possible. When Ruth

asked him why he was being so kind to her,

LOOK AT ALL THAT GRAIN!

he simply said, "I admire you. The **LOYALTY** you've shown to Naomi is AMAZING, as is your **COURAGE** in leaving your own family and country to live here with us. May God bless you for what you've done!" There was

another reason that Boaz did not admit to Ruth at first: he LIKED HER. Simple as that. Naomi could see it, though, so she encouraged them to spend more time together. And, in time, Boaz took the necessary steps to make Ruth his wife. It might sound **STRANGE** today but, in that place and time, when a man died, one of his relatives not only **INHERITED** his property but also the right to

THAT IS STRANGE!

marry the dead man's widow. This was so the name of the dead man could be carried on through whatever children were born. That person was called a REDEEMER, because he paid a **PRICE** for the land

and the rights that went with it. Unfortunately, Boaz wasn't the only redeemer of the land left by Naomi's husband and sons, but he could do **SOMETHING** about that. He went

to the man who *was* the closest redeemer, and Boaz asked if

he could buy the property instead. The man AGREED. Boaz

bought the land. And the right to wed Ruth went with it!

So the **LOYAL** foreign girl and the **RICH** farmer were married. And, yes, in the

best LOVE and ROMANCE tradition, they did seem to live (happily) ever after.

Ruth gave birth to a boy called **OBED**. And when Obed grew up and married, he

had a son called JESSE. And when Jesse grew up, he had many sons, including a

boy called David, who killed a GIANT and became a king—and was,

of course, a distant ancestor of a very special baby boy, who was laid

in a manger.

A VERY INTERRUPTIVE GOD

"SAMUEL!" someone called. **"SAMUEL!"** Samuel woke with a start.

The old priest **ELI**, who was nearly blind, must need his help. Samuel lived in the

tabernacle, the place where people came to worship God and where the ark

of the covenant was kept—the SIGN of God's presence. He had lived here

and helped Eli for as long as he could remember. That's because his mother had

prayed and prayed for a child, and when Samuel was born, she was so thankful

that she gave him back to God. Now Eli was calling him, and it was

late and it was dark. Only one special lamp shone in the

tabernacle, but Samuel didn't

need the LIGHT of the special lamp

PRETTY
BRIGHT!

to find his way. He knew every part of that tent by heart.

SAMUEL LIVES HERE!

And he made his way to Eli's side in no time.

"HERE I AM!" Samuel announced. The old priest **MUTTERED** and

SNUFFLED and shook himself awake. "I didn't call you," he grunted.

"Go back and lie down." "That was **STRANGE**,"

thought Samuel as he TIPTOED to his bed.

Things got stranger when the voice called again:

"SAMUEL!" Samuel went back to the priest. "You called me. Here I am!"

But the priest was not pleased to see him. Not pleased at all.

"I did not call you," Eli replied, more FIRMLY than the first

time. "Go and lie down." So Samuel

returned to his bed, glancing this way and that in case

the **SECRET** speaker was hiding somewhere. He crawled under the

covers, head buried beneath his arms. As he finally fell into a fitful sleep,

the **VOICE** called his name once more: "SAMUEL!" The

boy again RAN to Eli's side. Breathlessly, he repeated,

"You called me! Here I am!" This time, Eli

did not send Samuel back to his bed. **STARING** into the darkness, as if

 those old eyes could see something, Eli waited. Then, **SLOWLY**, he nodded.

"This has not happened for a very long time," he said.

"But I believe it is happening now. It is GOD'S VOICE

you hear. He is the one who is < calling > you. So the next time he

calls, simply say, 'Speak, **LORD**.

Your servant is **LISTENING**.'"

WOAH!

Slowly, Samuel went back to his bed,

wondering all the while if he would hear

the **VOICE** again. Sure enough, the minute he laid down his head,

he (heard) his name: **"SAMUEL! SAMUEL!"** "Speak, Lord," Samuel

whispered. "Your servant is listening." And God spoke. He told Samuel things

that night and then time and time again through the rest of Samuel's life.

And that is how he became God's SPOKESPERSON, God's MESSENGER,

 God's PROPHET. And that is why the name Samuel—

a name that was first whispered in the night—became famous

throughout the land of **ISRAEL**.

THERE ARE **LOTS** OF PEOPLE IN THE BIBLE WHO HAVE HEARD FROM GOD. CAN YOU NAME ANY?

SAMUEL'S STORY CONTINUES

HOW TO CHOOSE A KING

YEAR after **YEAR**, Samuel passed God's (messages) on to God's people. Year after year, they listened. But then, one year, they gave Samuel a MESSAGE to take back to God! "All the countries around us have kings," the people said. "Tell God that we want a KING too!" When Samuel heard this, he was not happy. And neither was God. *He* was meant to be the King of his people! "They are not rejecting you," God said to Samuel. "They are **REJECTING** me. Let them have what they want, but be sure to tell them what that means." So Samuel did. "A king will turn your sons into SOLDIERS," he told the people, "and your daughters into his SERVANTS. He will take a tenth of everything you have and use the money to pay his officials. He will lead you into

VERY TALL!

WAR." The people, however, were determined to have their way. So Samuel found a man named **SAUL**, handsome and strong and TALL. Taller than anyone else in the land,

98

in fact. Which meant that people were FORCED to look up to him. Which made him seem **VERY** kingly indeed.

Samuel made him king over Israel by pouring OIL on his head—a sign that God's Spirit had been given to him and was WORKING THROUGH him. And, for a while, Saul let God's Spirit do exactly that.

But the problem with being HANDSOME and STRONG and TALL, sometimes, is that it doesn't take long before you start relying on your own strength and POWER to get things done. And that's what happened to Really TALL Saul. He did things his own way. He stopped listening to Samuel. And, worst of all, he disobeyed God. So God told Samuel to find someone else to be king. Someone **SMALLER**,

MAYBE NOT THIS SMALL!

preferably, though God didn't make that clear to Samuel.

Not at first anyway. God did send him to BETHLEHEM, though, to the home of a man called JESSE (Ruth's grandson, remember?).

"One of his sons is the new king," God told Samuel. Seven sons stood with

Jesse when the prophet arrived, so Samuel took a **GOOD** look at each of them. The first son—TALL, HANDSOME ELIAB—seemed promising. "He looks very kingly," thought Samuel. But God had a different idea. "We've been here before," he whispered to his prophet. "I'm not interested in his **HEIGHT** or his **GOOD LOOKS** or anything else to do with his appearance I have already **REJECTED** him. I'm interested in what is going on in his heart!" One by one, Jesse's sons PARADED before the prophet, but God said no to each of them too. "You don't, erm, happen to have any more sons, do you?" asked Samuel. "As a matter of fact, I do," Jesse replied.

"David, the youngest, is out in the fields, watching

the sheep." The boy was sent for. And Samuel knew the

MOMENT he saw him that David was the one. "HUMBLER.

YOUNGER. BETTER," thought the prophet as he began to

understand. "Someone who will need to trust God and who won't try to

RULE on his own." So Samuel **POURED** the oil on David's head.

God's Spirit RUSHED on the boy. And, even though they didn't know it yet,

the people of Israel had a brand-new king!

HE'LL MAKE A GREAT KING

A GIANT STORY TO COME!

DINKY DAVID AND THE GINORMOUS GIANT

God's Spirit was no longer with Saul, because Samuel had **ANOINTED** David. Although Saul <u>still</u> sat on the throne, he was no longer God's chosen king. Without God's Spirit, an **EVIL** spirit now troubled Saul. "Music might help to calm you," his servants said. So Saul   LYRE sent them to find someone to play for him. They found a young shepherd who was skilled at playing the **LYRE**. In Bethlehem. In the house of Jesse. Yes, that shepherd was David, the very person chosen to (replace) the ailing king! Saul didn't know this, of course. When David played, the music **SOOTHED** his soul. "I like you," Saul said. "You will play for me and you will be my own personal armor bearer." David's eldest brothers, **ELIAB**, **ABINADAB**, and **SHAMMAH**, were soldiers in Israel's army.

One day, David's father sent him to them with some grain and bread. "Let me know how they're doing," he said. As it happened, they weren't doing well. In fact, the WHOLE army was trembling with FEAR because the Philistines had come to fight them. And they had a rather UNUSUAL soldier on their side. He stood more than 9 feet tall. His BRONZE coat weighed 125 pounds and he carried a spear nearly 26 feet long! His name was GOLIATH and, every morning, he would issue this challenge to the army of Israel: "Send someone to fight me! If he wins, we will be your servants. But if I win, you will serve us!" Not one soldier thought he stood a chance against this GIANT of a man. When David visited, he heard the challenge too. He asked, "What reward will the king give to the man

who kills the giant?" "**GREAT RICHES**,"

replied a soldier. "Oh, and the hand of his daughter in

marriage." "I'll do it, then," said David. The king called **DAVID** to his side.

"You're just a boy!" Saul said. "**YOUNG** and **INEXPERIENCED**. This

Goliath has been a soldier for years." "When a lion attacked my father's

sheep," David replied, "I grabbed it and killed it. I did the same with a **BEAR**.

God saved me from them both and will save me from this Philistine too!"

"Then take my armor," said Saul. But David had no experience with fighting

in armor. What he did have, though, was a (sling.) So he took it, gathered

5 stones, and set off to face the giant. Silence fell on the battlefield when

Goliath appeared. A silence broken by the giant's mocking **LAUGHTER**

when David marched out to meet him. "Am I a dog?" he snorted. "Is that why

you've sent this STICK of a boy to fight me? Come close,

then, and I'll feed your flesh to the **BEASTS** and **BIRDS!**"

But David answered, "You come with a **SWORD**, a

HE IS PRETTY STRONG!

104

JAVELIN, and a SPEAR, but I come in the name of the Lord of heaven's army. He will give me the victory. I will strike you down dead. Your body, not mine, will make a meal for the BIRDS and BEASTS. And everyone will know there is a GOD in Israel!" As the giant RUSHED toward him, David slipped a stone into his sling and let it fly. Small, like the boy himself, the stone struck Goliath

UH-OH!

between the eyes. And the

WHAT A SHOT!

giant fell to the ground. David grabbed Goliath's sword. With a mighty swing, he STRUCK off the giant's head and killed him dead! The Philistines ran. The soldiers of Israel CHEERED. David was a hero. But, better than that, everyone knew there was indeed a God in Israel!

DAVID'S MISTAKE

Saul refused to accept God's judgment and let David be king. But God

protected David. God helped David. And when Saul was finally defeated, David

reigned as king from the city of **JERUSALEM**. David loved God. He

TRUSTED God and PRAISED God. Until, one day, he didn't. His

army was away, fighting a war. As David was walking on the roof

of his house, he saw a **BEAUTIFUL** woman. He liked her and

he sent for her. And when she arrived, he loved BATHSHEBA in a

way that a man is supposed to love only his wife. But Bathsheba wasn't

his wife. She was the wife of one of his soldiers, **URIAH**, who was away

FIGHTING the war. When Bathsheba told King David that

she was expecting his baby, he did everything he could to

make people think the baby was Uriah's. He asked Uriah to

come back from the battle to spend the night with Bathsheba. He asked

AGAIN and AGAIN. But Uriah was a loyal soldier and refused to spend

106

WHY AM I IN THE FRONT?!

the night indoors while his comrades slept on the ground. So David decided to deal with his PROBLEM another way. He sent Uriah back into **BATTLE**. He told his commander to put Uriah right at the front, where the fighting was fiercest, then pull the other **SOLDIERS** back and leave Uriah to face the enemy alone. And that's how Uriah died. David didn't KILL Uriah with his own sword. But he caused that faithful soldier's **DEATH** as surely as if he had. When a respectable time had passed, David married Uriah's widow. And his problem was solved. NOT in God's eyes, though. God sent a prophet called **NATHAN** to visit David and tell him a story. "Once there was a man who owned many flocks of sheep," Nathan began. "His neighbor, however, had only ONE sheep—a **LITTLE** lamb that he'd raised by hand and fed from his table. One day, the

FINE DINING!

first man had a visitor and wanted to feed him a NICE

POOR LAMB!

meal. But instead of choosing one of the many sheep he

owned, he stole the second man's lamb instead. He KILLED

it, cooked it, and served it to his **VISITOR**. What should be done with

that first man, Your Majesty?" "That man must be punished!" David ROARED.

"Tell me who he is!" Nathan raised his finger, pointed it at the KING, and

whispered, "You. YOU ARE THE MAN. And God says that, because

Uriah died by the sword, the sword will PLAGUE your family

until you die, and your own child will RISE against you." David fell to

his knees.

JESUS SPOKE IN STORIES
CALLED PARABLES TOO!
CAN YOU REMEMBER
ANY OF THEM?

Sobbing, he cried, "It's true! I have SINNED against God." "God will forgive

your sin," Nathan said. "But, sadly, the baby you had with Bathsheba

will die." So David, who praised God in song, wrote a PSALM to

God to say (sorry) and to thank him for his forgiveness:

BECAUSE YOUR LOVE
IS FAITHFUL, LORD,
BE MERCIFUL TO ME. AND
BECAUSE YOUR MERCY
NEVER ENDS, WASH ME
AND CLEANSE ME AND
BLOT OUT MY SINS.

It looked like the end for David. But because God LISTENS to a heart that

is (sorry) and desperately wants to change, there was **MORE**, so much

MORE: a child of promise, David's descendant, who would one day grant

God's forgiveness to the owner of every sorry heart who trusts in him...

A WISE DECISION

Just as the prophet Nathan foretold, VIOLENCE and TROUBLE never left

David's household. Some of the king's sons led a rebellion against him to

take his **THRONE**. They failed and, in the end, one of David's other

sons, **SOLOMON**, was crowned king. But David was a difficult

act to follow and Solomon knew it. So, after his father's death,

Solomon went to GIBEON, a holy place, to make a   WISE
                                                    GUY!

sacrifice to God. That's where God spoke to him. "What can I give you?"

God asked. Solomon could have asked for anything—**RICHES**, **POWER**,

FAME. But Solomon knew that leading God's people wouldn't be easy, so

he said, "Lord God, you blessed my father David, even through hard times. Now

you have given his throne to me and what I need, more than ANYTHING, is

WISDOM to rule this land and lead your people." God was pleased

with Solomon's answer. "You could have asked for riches or power or fame,"

GOOD
ANSWER!

God said, "but because you have asked for **WISDOM**,

I will give you that and those other things too! Just stay **FAITHFUL**

to me and keep my commandments." So Solomon became **FAMOUS** not only for

his **RICHES** and his **POWER** but also for his **WISDOM**. One day,

women visited him. Two women who lived in the same house. One of them was

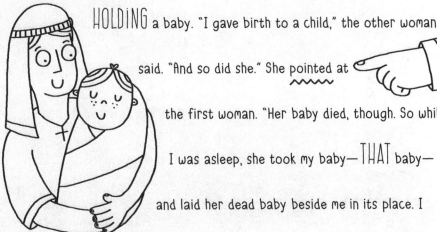

HOLDING a baby. "I gave birth to a child," the other woman

said. "And so did she." She pointed at

the first woman. "Her baby died, though. So while

I was asleep, she took my baby—THAT baby—

and laid her dead baby beside me in its place. I

knew—as soon as I woke—that the baby beside me wasn't mine, but now she

won't GIVE me my baby back!" The first woman shook her head and said,

"This is my baby! This has always been my baby!" So Solomon did

something very **WISE**. And very scary. He asked for a sword.

"You both say the baby belongs to you," he said. "So we'll cut the

baby in **TWO** and each of you can leave here with half a baby."

"No!" cried the second woman. "I would rather she have my baby than see him cut in two!" "Do it," GRUNTED the first woman. "That way neither of us will have him." Solomon had his answer. "Only a mother would rather give her son **AWAY** than see him killed," he said. "Give the baby to the woman who brought the complaint." That's not the only **WISE** thing Solomon did, of

course. He wrote hundreds of proverbs—wise sayings that taught people the **BEST** way to live. And he was charged by God with building the temple—the GREAT and **BEAUTIFUL** building that replaced the tabernacle tent and held

the ark of the covenant. For afterward, the people of Israel would go there to worship God and offer **SACRIFICES** to him. But, sadly, Solomon did not keep his promises to God. He married women from other countries— **700** of them! And he not only let his wives worship their foreign gods but built places around the country for the

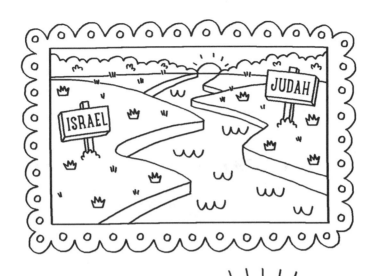

worship of those gods as well. And Solomon WORSHIPED them too! So

God divided Solomon's kingdom in half, a lot like Solomon had threatened to

DIVIDE the baby. The **NORTHERN** tribes became the kingdom of

Israel. The **SOUTHERN** tribes were called the kingdom of Judah. And for

all his WISDOM and his WEALTH, Solomon could not keep his country

together because he had turned away from the God who had given him

wisdom in the first place.

OH NO! WHAT WILL HAPPEN NEXT?

 # NO RAIN FORECAST

After Solomon's kingdom split into the kingdom of Israel, up NORTH, and the

kingdom of Judah, down SOUTH, there were (lots) of kings. A few were

GOOD. Some were very **BAD**. But one of the worst was King **AHAB**, who

ruled Israel. He was married to Queen JEZEBEL, from the land of

the Philistines, who worshiped a false god called Baal. **BAAL** was a

"FERTILITY GOD." People believed that if they made sacrifices to Baal,

their crops would GROW and they would prosper. But it

wasn't true. Baal was nothing more than an idol—just statues

set up on the hills—with no **POWER** at all. But because

Jezebel was very persuasive and she was the king's wife,

she was also very POWERFUL. She used that power to

set up those idols across Israel and to hurt anyone who disagreed with

her—anyone who worshiped the Lord, the God of Israel, who had rescued

his people and led them to a land they could call their OWN. A God who

was **REAL** and could actually do something. Not

something IDLE, like an idol, like Baal. So God decided to

act. He sent his prophet **ELIJAH** to King Ahab.

"God says no rain will fall," declared Elijah, "until you stop worshiping Baal."

NOT GOOD!

Ahab refused to change. So the rain stopped falling. For **3** long years!

The drought led to a **FAMINE**. The famine grew worse and

worse. And when Elijah went to see Ahab again, the king was

FURIOUS with him. "You've turned your back on God," Elijah

said, "disobeyed his commandments and worshiped Baal. This drought is

your fault! Send your prophets of Baal to Mount Carmel and we'll see who

worships the true God." Up to the mountaintop trooped the prophets of

Baal—four hundred and fifty of them. The people of Israel **FOLLOWED**

to see what would happen. "You WORSHIP the Lord God one minute,"

Elijah cried out to the people, "and the next you worship

Baal. The time has come to choose. We'll have a **CONTEST**.

If Baal wins, worship Baal. But if the Lord PROVES himself

to be the true God, then he is the one you must follow."

Elijah called for two bulls to be slaughtered. "Cut your bull

into pieces," he said to the prophets of Baal. "Lay it on your altar.

Then call for your god to send FIRE from heaven to burn up the bull."

The prophets of Baal did as Elijah said. From morning until noon, they called

on Baal. But nothing happened. NADA. "Maybe your god is sleeping," Elijah

HOPE HE FLUSHED!

suggested. "Or he's away on a journey. Or in the bathroom."

So the prophets of Baal cried out even LOUDER. Still

nothing happened. And when they'd exhausted themselves,

Elijah prepared his bull. He built an altar of 12 stones,

one for each of the tribes of Israel. He stacked wood on the

stones. He put the pieces of the bull on the wood. Then

he dug a TRENCH around the altar. And he poured

water— PRECIOUS water in the midst of a

drought!—over **EVERYTHING**, until it flowed down into the trench. "Lord God," he prayed, "show your people that you are the (true) God and I am your prophet. Send FIRE and turn them back to you." As soon as Elijah had finished, fire fell from heaven and burnt up the **BULL**, the **WOOD**, the STONES, the WATER! The people fell on their faces and shouted, "The Lord, he is God!"

They chased the **PROPHETS** of Baal and killed them. Then, and only then, did it begin to rain.

FINALLY, RAIN!

117

ISAIAH'S BURNING VISION

God sent prophets like Elijah to speak to the >**BAD**< kings of Israel. But

although there were a few ˙GOOD˙ rulers in the southern kingdom of Judah,

there were plenty of bad ones as well. So God had to send prophets to

them too, to tell them to **WORSHIP** the true God and not pick on the

poor. One of the most famous of those prophets was called ISAIAH. In the

A MUCH LONGER ROBE THAN THIS!

year that King Uzziah died, Isaiah was in the temple in Jerusalem that

Solomon had built. While he worshiped there, he had a

VISION. He saw God! God was lifted up, in

the air. God was sitting on a throne. God was

wearing a robe. The bottom of that robe flowed down

from the throne, fold by unfolding fold, until it filled the temple. Above God

stood the **SERAPHIM**, angelic beings that burned as BRIGHT as firelight

(that's what their name means). They each had **6** wings. With two

wings they covered their faces. With two they covered their feet.

And, yeah, with the last two wings they flew. And they weren't **SILENT**,

these seraphim. As they FLAPPED and flew, they called out to one another

in a chorus of praise to God:

> HOLY, HOLY, HOLY IS THE GOD OF HEAVEN'S ARMIES! THE EARTH IS FILLED WITH HIS GLORY.

The temple **SHOOK** at the sound of the seraphims'

call, right to its FOUNDATIONS. The place filled

with smoke. And what did Isaiah do, in the midst

of the seraphim and the smoke, surrounded by thundering voices and

CRUMBLING floors? At the foot of the throne of God? He cried out,

"Woe is me!" That's what he did. And who wouldn't? "I'm in trouble!" he cried.

"For my eyes have seen God himself. The King. The Lord of heaven's armies!

Yet I'm a man with **UNCLEAN** lips. And I'm surrounded by people whose lips are unclean too!" Which was pretty much Isaiah's way of saying that he and

the others in his land had done lots of WRONG things.

And just as he was "woe-ing" and TREMBLING and

wondering what God would do with a sinner like him, Isaiah saw

something else. One of the seraphim GRABBED a set of tongs

and pulled a red-hot COAL out of the fire that burned on the altar. Then HOT STUFF!

he flew straight toward Isaiah, holding that coal before him. You

can only imagine Isaiah's thoughts as that flaming, heavenly

being drew NEARER and NEARER. I suspect "I'M DOOMED!"

comes pretty close. But he wasn't. Not at all. The seraphim touched

the burning coal to Isaiah's LIPS (all right, that can't have been

EEEK! pleasant) but what the seraphim said was: "This coal from the altar

has touched your lips. Now your GUILT has been taken away and your sins

WHOSE VOICE IS THAT? paid for." Then Isaiah heard a voice. A voice from

the throne. The VOICE of God himself. "Whom shall I send?"

the voice asked. "Who will go for us?" And Isaiah **HEARD**

another voice—his own: "I'm here. Send me!" From then

on, for **50** years and more, Isaiah passed

God's **MESSAGES** on to his people. Messages

warning them to turn back to God and PROMISING

them God's help. And a message, specially for people in the

ages to come, of hope about a savior who would bear the punishment for

all the wrong things anyone would ever do. About a **SACRIFICIAL** lamb

of a man whose pain would erase the wounds of the world. A message,

hundreds of years before his birth, about a man called **JESUS**.

A SPECIAL DISCOVERY

JOSIAH became king of Judah when he was 8 years old. That was far too YOUNG to qualify for most jobs, much less ruling an entire nation.

The thing is, though, Josiah loved God and wanted to honor God. And when he was twenty-six, he happened on an **OPPORTUNITY** to do just that. The temple—the one that Solomon had built—was a bit of a **WRECK**. So Josiah sent SHAPHAN, one of his officials, to speak to **HILKIAH**, the high priest. Shaphan told Hilkiah to take the money the people had given as an offering in the temple, and hire workers—stonemasons, carpenters, and the like—to repair what needed to be repaired. So that's what the high priest did. ROTTEN timber was replaced. CRACKED stones were too. It was a **BIG** job! But in the midst of all that work, Hilkiah found something. Something that made him very **EXCITED** indeed. No, it wasn't gold.

NEW TIMBER!

122

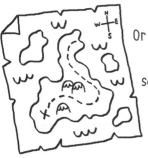

Or precious stones. Or a **TREASURE** map. It was

something much more VALUABLE. It was, in fact, a book.

And not just any book. It was the book of the law, the

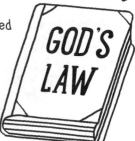

GOD'S LAW

law that God had given to Moses and that had been passed

down through the years; the law that God's people were

meant to **FOLLOW**. Hilkiah read the book to Shaphan.

Shaphan READ the book to the king. And when

King Josiah heard the words in the book, he

TORE his clothes—which is what people did in those

days when they were UPSET. Why was he upset? Because

the book said pretty clearly that **DISASTER** would

fall on God's (people) if they did not honor him and

MUST BE REALLY UPSET!

treat each other well. And, largely because they'd had a bunch of evil kings,

they had not obeyed God's laws for a very long time.

Fortunately, there was a PROPHET in town, a woman

THERE'VE BEEN QUITE A FEW EVIL KINGS!

called **HULDAH**. Shaphan and Hilkiah and several other officials

went to see her. They told her about the book and how the **KING** had

reacted, and this is what she said to them: "Because God's people have not

obeyed him and have WORSHIPED other gods, the disaster promised in the

book will FALL on this land. But since Josiah has WEPT and said he is

sorry and has **HUMBLED** himself before God, he will enjoy a

long and peaceful life and will not live to see that disaster." When

Josiah heard Huldah's words, he was GRATEFUL. Then he

set out to make his "sorry" words a reality. He began by

calling the people together and reading out the words of the

book so that everyone could hear. Then he sent his men to tear

down every place that was used to worship

NO MORE FALSE GODS!

Baal and **EVERY** other false god. He

burned up the things they used on their

own ALTARS. And he burned up the priests of

those **FALSE** gods as well! Then, for the first time in a very long time, he

led his people in **CELEBRATING** the Passover. After getting rid

of the false gods, they remembered what the TRUE God had done—how he

had rescued their ancestors from slavery in Egypt and led them through the

desert to a place they could call **HOME**. And so Josiah was listed in the

books that followed as a GOOD KING —a king who followed God, straight

down a straight path.

JOSIAH,
THE GOOD
KING!

 # A PROPHET TO THE RESCUE! →

While Josiah was king of Judah, and even before his workers found the book of the law, God appointed JEREMIAH to be his prophet. "Before you were in your mother's womb, I knew you," God told him. "And before you were born I had already decided that you would be my prophet, my **SPOKESMAN** to the world!" Jeremiah was probably only **17** when he heard those WORDS. He said to God, "I'm still young! I won't know what to say!"

God had heard this **EXCUSE** before. From an old man who stood before a burning bush.

CAN YOU REMEMBER HIS NAME?

"Don't worry about your age," God assured Jeremiah. "I will give you the WORDS and you will pass them on. But some people will not like what you have to say. So when they **THREATEN**

you, don't be afraid. I will be there to rescue you!" Then God **TOUCHED**

Jeremiah's mouth and said, "Today I put my 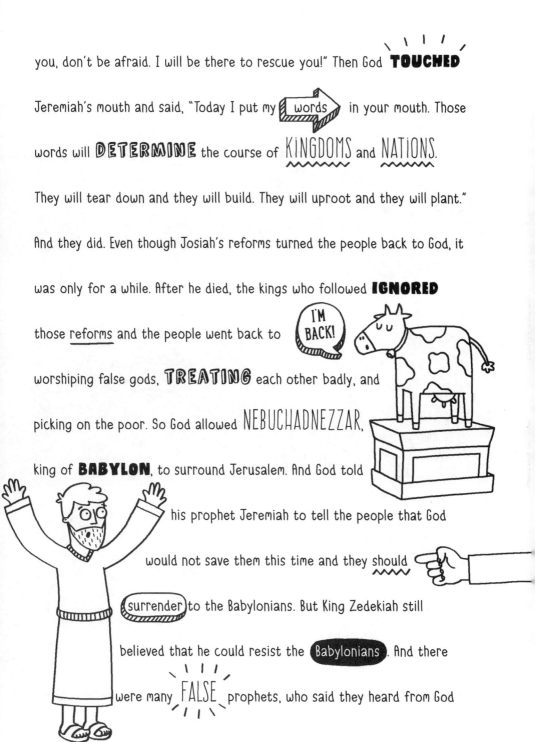 words in your mouth. Those

words will **DETERMINE** the course of KINGDOMS and NATIONS.

They will tear down and they will build. They will uproot and they will plant."

And they did. Even though Josiah's reforms turned the people back to God, it

was only for a while. After he died, the kings who followed **IGNORED**

those reforms and the people went back to (I'M BACK!)

worshiping false gods, **TREATING** each other badly, and

picking on the poor. So God allowed NEBUCHADNEZZAR,

king of **BABYLON**, to surround Jerusalem. And God told

his prophet Jeremiah to tell the people that God

would not save them this time and they should

(surrender) to the Babylonians. But King Zedekiah still

believed that he could resist the (Babylonians). And there

were many FALSE prophets, who said they heard from God

but didn't, who were **HAPPY** to encourage him. Still, Jeremiah was clear:

"God wants you to **SURRENDER**. For by doing so, you will save your

people from much suffering!" He announced the <u>SAME</u> thing to the people:

"Leave the city. Surrender to the Babylonians and you **WILL** live!" This

worried the king and his officials. "Jeremiah is frightening the people and

weakening their resolve to fight!" they argued. "Let us deal with him!" The

king agreed, and his **OFFICIALS** arrested Jeremiah and dumped him into a

 cistern, where he sank into the at the bottom.

One of the king's servants, an Ethiopian called

EBED-MELECH, heard what had happened and went to

tell Zedekiah. "Your Majesty," he said, "you must do

something or Jeremiah will die!" Maybe, deep **DOWN** inside, Zedekiah knew that

Jeremiah really was God's spokesman. So he gave Ebed-Melech

men and told him to pull the prophet out of the cistern. Ebed-Melech knew

this would be hard. The mud at the bottom was **THICK** and **STICKY**, and it

SMELLY!

would take a lot of **STRENGTH**. So

he gathered up some of the king's OLD

clothes. Then he tied them to the end of

a rope and lowered it down to Jeremiah. "Wrap the clothes

between your body and the ropes," he called. "That way the

ropes won't **RUB** you when we pull you out." So that's what

Jeremiah did. And God's words to him came true: "People will

threaten you. Don't be afraid. I will **PROTECT** you." And

when the king called for him again, Jeremiah's message was

the same: "SURRENDER." For God had put his words

into Jeremiah's mouth and Jeremiah was determined

to tell the truth. Sadly, the king didn't listen. When Jerusalem was

eventually conquered, just as Jeremiah said it would be, Jeremiah survived

and went with his CAPTIVE people to live as an **EXILE** in Babylon.

 # THE FIERY FURNACE

Nebuchadnezzar, the king of Babylon, was SMART. Whenever he conquered

a country, he brought the brightest, best young people from that land to

Babylon and gave them special treatment. He sent them to school and tried

his (best) to turn those exiles into GOOD

Babylonians. He **HOPED** it would help them

settle in their new home and keep the people in their old, conquered lands

from turning against him. That's what happened to HANANIAH, MISHAEL,

AZARIAH, and DANIEL when Nebuchadnezzar destroyed Jerusalem and

conquered the kingdom of Judah. They were given Babylonian names:

SHADRACH, MESHACH, ABEDNEGO, and **BELTESHAZZAR**.

They were enrolled in the king's school. They were fed from the king's own

 menu—and that's when things got TRICKY. It may

have been that some of the king's food was on the list

of ANIMALS that God's people were not allowed to eat

or that some of the food had been **OFFERED** to false gods. Whatever the case, the four young men were determined to be FAITHFUL to their

LOOKS TASTY!

God, so they refused to eat what was placed before them. Ashpenaz, the king's servant in charge of training them, was not happy. "If you fall ill," he cried, "the king will **BLAME** me and I'll be in big trouble" "Don't worry," Daniel (well, Belteshazzar) assured him. "We will eat the food we think is RIGHT for us. The young men from the other countries can eat the king's fare. And after **10** days, we shall see who fares the best." Ten days passed and, sure enough, Daniel and his friends were **HEALTHY** and fit!

So they were allowed to eat what they liked. And when their education was finished, they were given IMPORTANT jobs in the kingdom. One day, the king ordered all his officials to stand before a **GIANT** golden idol. "When the band begins to play," the king's messenger announced, "everyone must bow down before the statue. Any official who doesn't will be **THROWN**  into a FURNACE filled with fire!" But Shadrach,

Meshach, and Abednego could not bow down before that idol.

Back home, they'd learned that there was only **1** God and he

was the only one they could worship. So when the rest of the

crowd bowed, they stood. It wasn't long before some other

officials, who were **JEALOUS** of their **WISDOM** and

positions, told the king. Nebuchadnezzar was furious. He gave them

another chance to bow before the statue, but they still refused. "Throw us

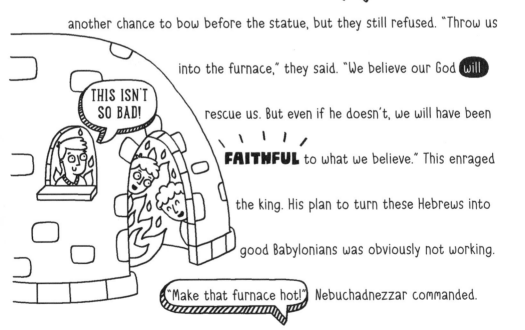

into the furnace," they said. "We believe our God will

rescue us. But even if he doesn't, we will have been

FAITHFUL to what we believe." This enraged

the king. His plan to turn these Hebrews into

good Babylonians was obviously not working.

"Make that furnace hot!" Nebuchadnezzar commanded.

So his servants did, making it **7** times hotter than it had ever been before.

So hot, in fact, that the soldiers who threw Shadrach, Meshach, and Abednego

into the furnace were **BURNED** up where they stood. Things were different

for the three friends, however. Nebuchadnezzar rose and LOOKED into the

NOT ONE SINGLE BURNT HAIR! fire. "They are unharmed!"

he cried. "And there is someone in there with

them. A fourth person who looks like a **SON** of

the gods!" So he called to the men, "Come out!" And out of the fire the three

friends walked, not a SINGED hair or a SMOKY smell among them! "Your

God has saved you!" the king announced. "So I declare that, from this day

forward, no one in my kingdom shall say a bad word about the God of

Shadrach, Meshach, and Abednego. For he is a **GREAT** God, who rescues

those who trust him!"

NEBUCHADNEZZAR'S DREAM

King Nebuchadnezzar couldn't sleep. He kept DREAMING a dream that kept

him up at night. So he sent for his **MAGICIANS** and **WISE MEN** and

SORCERERS. "Tell me what my dream means," he ordered them. Quite

naturally, they asked, "Please, O King, tell us what you dreamed." "Oh no," he

replied. "I'm not PLAYING that game. If I tell you my dream, you can

make up any old meaning to explain it. Tell me what I dreamed first, to show

that you REALLY know what you're doing. Then tell

me what it means. And, by the way," he added, "if you

cannot do this, I will **DESTROY** every one of your

houses and tear you to pieces, limb from limb!" "B-but, Your Majesty!" they

cried. "What you ask is impossible! It's a job for the gods. There's **NOT** a

PERSON on earth who can do this!" So King Nebuchadnezzar sent

out an order that every magician and wise man and sorcerer in the

land should be torn to pieces, limb from

limb. Daniel and his **3** friends—Shadrach, Meshach, and Abednego—were

wise men too. So when the **CAPTAIN** of the guard came to kill them,

Daniel asked to see the king. "Give me some time," he said. "I will tell **you**

both your **DREAM** and its meaning." The king agreed and Daniel went to his

friends and asked them to pray for him. Then, in the night, God showed the

dream and its MEANING to him. So Daniel went to see the king. "Please don't

kill the wise men," he begged. "I have the answer. Or, rather, my **GOD** has the

answer and he has shown it to me."

WHO ELSE HELPED
A RULER WITH HIS
DREAMS? HINT: HE
HAD VERY SNAZZY
DRESS SENSE...

"Tell me," the king replied, "what was my dream?" "You saw a statue," Daniel

began. "**BIG** and **BRIGHT** and **FRIGHTENING!** Its head was made

of gold. Its arms and chest were silver, its belly and thighs bronze. Its legs

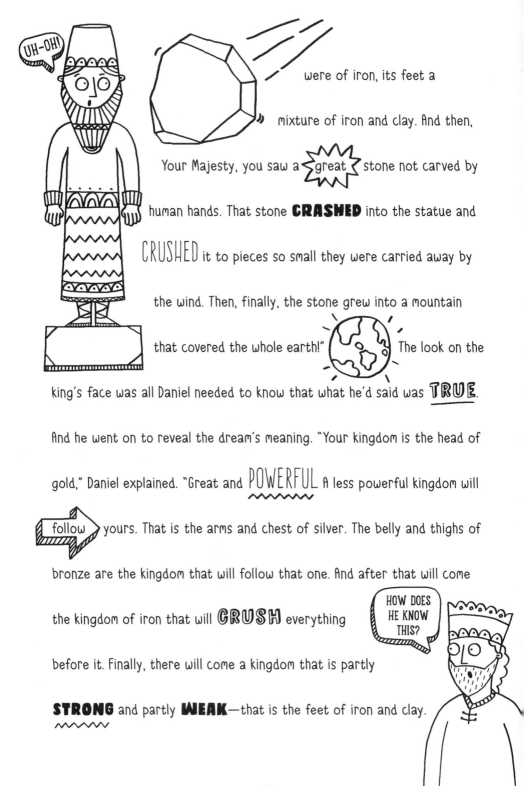

UH-OH!

were of iron, its feet a mixture of iron and clay. And then, Your Majesty, you saw a great stone not carved by human hands. That stone **CRASHED** into the statue and CRUSHED it to pieces so small they were carried away by the wind. Then, finally, the stone grew into a mountain that covered the whole earth!" The look on the king's face was all Daniel needed to know that what he'd said was **TRUE**.

And he went on to reveal the dream's meaning. "Your kingdom is the head of gold," Daniel explained. "Great and POWERFUL. A less powerful kingdom will follow yours. That is the arms and chest of silver. The belly and thighs of bronze are the kingdom that will follow that one. And after that will come the kingdom of iron that will **CRUSH** everything before it. Finally, there will come a kingdom that is partly **STRONG** and partly **WEAK**—that is the feet of iron and clay.

HOW DOES HE KNOW THIS?

And in the days of that kingdom, God himself will set up a kingdom that will crush every other kingdom and FILL the earth. That is the stone that grows into a mountain." When King Nebuchadnezzar heard Daniel's interpretation, he fell on his face before him. "Surely your God is a GREAT God!" he cried. "A God who **REVEALS** mysteries!" With that, he honored Daniel with GIFTS and made him ruler over the whole province of Babylon! Shadrach, Meshach, and Abednego were given promotions too. And the 4 men who had come to Babylon as captives were put in charge of those who had captured them, simply because they were FAITHFUL to their God and trusted in his power.

A ROARSOME STORY NEXT!

TONIGHT'S MENU: DANIEL

King Nebuchadnezzar's dream came true, possibly sooner than he expected.

During the reign of his son, **BELSHAZZAR**, Babylon was conquered by

the Persians and the Medes, and DARIUS became king. Daniel, however,

survived it all. In fact, his reputation as a man of wisdom brought him to

the attention of the new king, and Darius made him one of the most

POWERFUL officials in the land. Daniel did his job well. And when word

LOOK, HE'S PRAYING AGAIN! went around that the king was about to

put Daniel in charge of every other official, they were

overcome with **JEALOUSY**. "We must find a way to

stop him!" they plotted. But Daniel was so HONEST and

FAITHFUL that they could not find any fault with him. So they decided, in

the end, to use Daniel's faithfulness against him. They knew that Daniel

prayed to his God **EVERY** day, so they went to the king with an

idea they were sure would please him. "Your Majesty," they said, "you are **AMAZING** and we want everyone in your kingdom to recognize that. So we would like you to pass a law saying (YUM!)

that, for **30** days, no one should offer up PRAYERS

to anyone but you. Furthermore, anyone who disobeys this law will be thrown into a den filled with **LIONS**." The king agreed. The law was passed. Daniel disobeyed it, of course, because he was, as his >ENEMIES< had predicted, **FAITHFUL** to his God. Right away he was arrested and brought before King Darius. And, as much as it upset the king, there was nothing he could do to (save) his FAVORITE official. "The rules are clear," Daniel's enemies explained. "You cannot change a law that you yourself have

passed." So Daniel was brought to the lions'

den. But, just before he was lowered to his

death, the king came to him and said

quietly, "May the God you serve deliver

you." Then the king had Daniel lowered into

the den and **COMMANDED** that a stone be placed across the top so there

I HOPE HE'S OK.

was no chance of escape—a stone he marked with his own royal seal. Darius returned to his palace. And did not EAT. And did not SLEEP. Daniel spent the night with the **HUNGRY** lions. As soon as the (SUN) rose, as soon as he could see to make his way, King Darius went to the den.

A (den) that he was sure had become a TOMB for Daniel. In anguish, he cried out, "Daniel! Daniel! Has the God you serve saved you?" And up from the den rose a voice in return. "He has, Your Majesty! He sent his **ANGEL** to shut the lions' (mouths). I am unharmed, for I have not sinned before my God. And I meant no **HARM** to you, either, when I prayed to him and not you." Delighted, Darius called for his men to lift Daniel out of the den. Then, FURIOUS, he ordered them to drop Daniel's enemies down into the den in his place. King Darius sent out a **PROCLAMATION** throughout his kingdom,

PRAISING Daniel's God. Daniel prospered under Darius and under

the king who followed him as well. And they all lived **HAPPILY** ever after.

Even the lions, who **ENJOYED** a lovely breakfast!

REBUILDING A CITY IN FIFTY-TWO DAYS

Seventy years. That's how long God's people were in EXILE—away from

the land God had given them. The Babylonians, who had conquered them, were

themselves conquered by the Persians. And the (Persian) king at that time,

CYRUS, gave permission for God's people, the Israelites, to finally

WHAT A MESS!

→ return to their land. Bit by bit, the

people returned home. Their

beloved city, **JERUSALEM**, was in ruins. They did their best, but it

was hard for God's people to make everything right again. They rebuilt the

temple, but the city itself was a much (harder) job. Its walls had been

KNOCKED down, its gates BURNED by fire. And even though they tried to

rebuild, it was a struggle. Many more years passed. One Persian

king followed another. During the reign of **ARTAXERXES**,

a man called **NEHEMIAH**, who was the king's cupbearer,

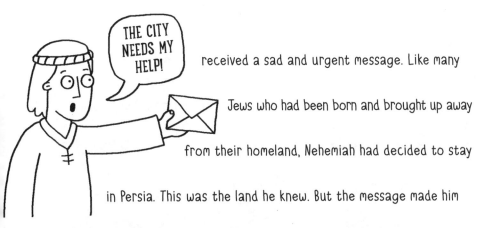

THE CITY NEEDS MY HELP!

received a sad and urgent message. Like many

Jews who had been born and brought up away

from their homeland, Nehemiah had decided to stay

in Persia. This was the land he knew. But the message made him

RECONSIDER that decision. It described the TERRIBLE state of

Jerusalem and asked for whatever help Nehemiah could give. So Nehemiah

prayed to God. Then he went to see the king. "Allow

me to go to the land of my fathers," he said. "Grant me

safe passage back to Jerusalem. And, if it pleases Your Majesty,

could you give me TIMBER from your forests as well, to rebuild the gates of

OH NO!

the city?" King Artaxerxes gave his BLESSING to

Nehemiah's MISSION and plenty of timber too!

So off the cupbearer went. When he arrived

in Jerusalem, he rode his horse around the ruined walls

to see the DAMAGE for himself.

It was worse than he'd feared. So he organized the people into groups, according to their families, to rebuild both the **WALLS** and the **GATES**. The work went well. The work went QUICKLY. But there were other people in that land who did not want to see the city rebuilt—enemies who knew that a **STRONG**, walled city would make God's people hard to defeat. So they (threatened) the workers and even planned to murder Nehemiah. Did that slow God's people down? It did not. It made them WORK even harder. And work smarter too. To defend themselves, they worked side by side, with a **TROWEL** in one hand

WE'RE SMARTER THAN YOU!

and a **SWORD** in the other! They worked so hard, in fact, that the whole job was completed in just

fifty-two days! And when they had finished, they read God's law out loud and praised him for his FAITHFULNESS and his **HELP**.

They were back in their homeland. Back in their temple.

And they were determined to be the people God wanted them to be! Hundreds of years passed. But that **SPECIAL** child, born from God's chosen family, born to be the blessing God had promised, born to **CRUSH** the serpent's head, was nowhere to be seen. And that's because there was MORE, so much MORE to come...

MORE AMAZING STORIES THIS WAY!

NEW TESTAMENT

THE IMPOSSIBLE PROMISE

BOOM! Out of nowhere, there he was. An angel.

And **MARY** was TERRIFIED! Maybe it was the suddenness of his arrival. Maybe it was the shock of the surprise. Maybe it was because he wasn't a "fat baby with wings" but a **BRIGHT**, shiny, otherworldly creature sent down from the throne of God. Or maybe it had to do with what he said: "Hello, favored one! God is with you." Mary was simply a young woman from a little town called NAZARETH, in the region of Galilee. She had never expected anything like this to happen to

SURPRISE!

her. What did the angel mean? What was this all about? She was confused and troubled, to say the least. And the angel, Gabriel, understood that.

"Don't be afraid," he assured her. "This is a good thing! God is **PLEASED** with you and wants to do something **AMAZING** for you. So, here is

148

what's going to happen: you will give birth to a

son and you will name him **JESUS**. He will be

great. In fact, he will be called the Son of God.

God will give him the throne of his ancestor, **DAVID**. He will put him in

charge of everyone descended from Jacob. And his kingdom will last forever!"

It was the PROMISE! The promise to Eve of a child to crush the serpent's head.

The promise to Abraham that, through his family, God would one day bless the

THERE'S JUST ONE THING...

world. The promise **FINALLY** come true. And it

sounded amazing. But Mary had a practical question.

Very practical. Her parents had arranged for her to

marry a man named JOSEPH, but there hadn't been a wedding

yet. So she asked, quite rightly, "I'm a virgin. How will I give

birth to a son?" And, quite rightly, Gabriel gave her an answer.

A **MYSTERIOUS** answer guaranteed to **SURPRISE** her

even more: "God's Holy Spirit will come upon you. His **POWER** will cover you. So your son will be **HOLY** too—the Son of God!

It sounds **INCREDIBLE**, I know, but your cousin Elizabeth is having

a baby. She's **6** months pregnant, in fact. And, as you know, no one

thought she could have kids at her age. But God can do ANYTHING.

Even something that everyone else thinks is impossible."

REMEMBER ME?

ELIZABETH'S MIRACLE SOUNDS FAMILIAR! DO YOU REMEMBER SOMETHING SIMILAR HAPPENING IN THE OLD TESTAMENT?

"Then let God do this '**IMPOSSIBLE**' thing for me," Mary replied.

"I will be his servant and do what he has asked." And with that, just as

SUDDENLY as he had come, the angel disappeared.

WONDER WHAT
WILL HAPPEN
NEXT...

ONE VERY LONG JOURNEY

BETHLEHEM

It was the last thing Joseph wanted to hear. Mary, the woman he had

PROMISED to marry, was expecting a baby. And there was no way

the baby was his. What could he do? She had BROKEN her promise,

broken the legal engagement that her family had made with him.

And, worst of all, she had broken his heart. He could have

embarrassed her and made a big deal out of what she had done. But

Joseph was a **GOOD** man and a **KIND** man. So he decided to end their

engagement but to do it quietly. But before he could put his **PLAN** into

action, —**BOOM!**—out of nowhere, he had a visit from an angel,

just like Mary did! The angel came to him at night, in a dream. "JOSEPH!"

the angel said. "Don't be afraid to marry Mary. She has not been

unfaithful to you. The baby she is expecting is there

by the power of God's own **HOLY SPIRIT**.

She is going to give birth to a son. And God wants you to

152

call him Jesus, because just like his name means, he will **RESCUE** his people

from their sins!" Do you remember Isaiah, the prophet? God told him that this

would happen. And this is what Isaiah wrote, HUNDREDS and HUNDREDS of

years before Mary and Joseph were

born: "Look and see and wonder! A virgin

will expect a baby. She will give **BIRTH** to

a son. And they will call him Immanuel

(a name that means 'God is with us')."

When Joseph woke up, he did exactly what the angel told him and

took Mary as his wife. But then—BOOM!—another surprise! The Roman ruler

Augustus wanted to find out how many people were in his vast empire. So he

YES. EVERYONE! ordered everyone under his control to

RETURN to their

hometown to be counted. Joseph was from

BETHLEHEM, the town where King

David once lived. In fact, King David was one of Joseph's ANCESTORS.

DO YOU REMEMBER ANY STORIES FROM THE OLD TESTAMENT ABOUT KING DAVID?

So he and Mary had to TRAVEL to be counted in the **CENSUS**. It was

 miles or so. And, despite what you might have seen in your

school nativity play, they probably had to walk (sorry, little donkey!).

I'LL STICK TO THE ACTING!

It can't have been easy. When they arrived, they

needed a place to **STAY**, but so did all of Joseph's

other relatives. And by the time they got to Bethlehem, all

the NICE upstairs rooms, where families

SORRY ABOUT THE SMELL!

usually kept their guests, were full. So Mary

and Joseph had to stay where the (animals) were kept. And it was there,

among the animals and the straw, that Mary gave birth to **JESUS**. So she

wrapped him in cloths and laid him in a **MANGER**.

A FLASH MOB OF ANGELS

BAAAA!

Nearby, on the hills outside Bethlehem, there were shepherds GUARDING their flocks of sheep. The night was still. The stars were shining. All was quiet, apart from the odd sleepy **BAAAAA**. And then—**BOOM!**—that angel appeared again. And the light that surrounded him surrounded the shepherds too. It turned the night BRIGHT as white and gave those shepherds an almighty fright! "Don't be afraid!" the angel said. Just like he'd said to Mary. Just like he'd said to Joseph. "The news I bring you is

IS THIS A DREAM?

GOOD! And it will fill everyone who hears it with joy! Today, in Bethlehem, in David's city, your savior was born. That's right. The **MESSIAH,** the one God promised you. The one you

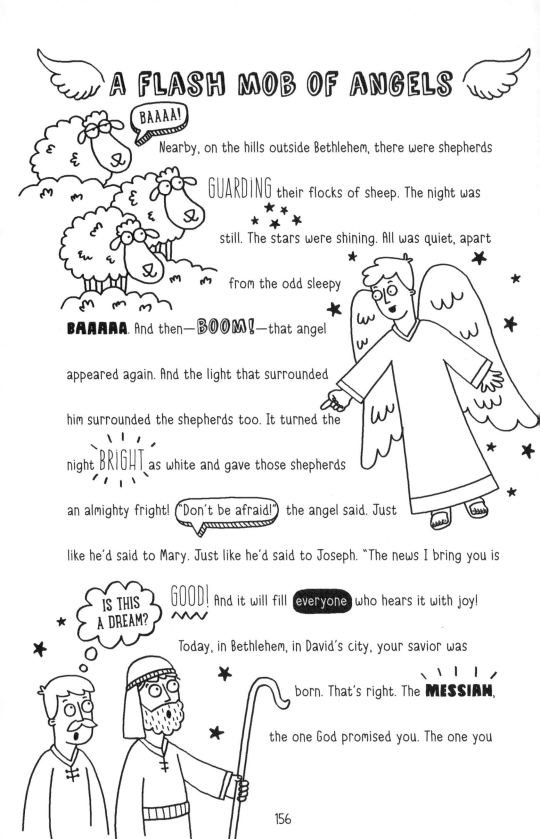

156

have been **WAITING** for, **YEAR** after **YEAR** after **YEAR**. He's here!

And this is the 'sign' that points to him so you will know for sure that

you've found him: look for a BABY, wrapped in cloths fit for a newborn,

lying in a manger." And when the angel had said that—**BOOM!**—a

sky full of angels joined him: a crowd, a multitude, a heavenly host!

Like an otherworldly CHOIR or a flash mob sent

from heaven, they shouted out their praises to God:

"Glory to God, who reigns on HIGH, and peace to those

on earth who please him!" Then—**BOOM!**—away they went, as suddenly as

they had appeared. The shepherds, still shaking, said to one another, "God

THERE HE IS!

has told us this **AMAZING** thing! Let's go

to Bethlehem and see!" So off they went,

HURRYING, RUNNING, RACING to the place

the angel had revealed to

them. And there was Mary.

There was Joseph. And there was a BABY, just like the

angel had said, lying in a manger. So the shepherds told Mary and Joseph

EVERYTHING the angel had said to them about the baby—how he

was the Messiah, God's long-promised one, finally come to his people. And

Mary kept those words, like a TREASURE, in her heart,

to wonder and to ponder over, in the **DAYS** and

WEEKS and **YEARS** to come. Then back to the

hills the shepherds went, praising God for all they

had seen and heard. No longer quiet, no longer still, but **SHOUTING** and **SINGING** like angels.

THE STAR-WATCHERS

BOOM! BOOM! BOOM! The star-watchers knocked on the door to the palace—the palace of HEROD, king of the Jews (which is what God's people were now called). And when they stood before him, they gave him news that landed like an **EXPLOSION** on his

ears. "Can you tell us where we can find the newborn King of the Jews? We saw his star RISE in the night skies and we have come to worship him." It was all King Herod could do to keep himself from **EXPLODING** with RAGE. He was the

A VERY ANGRY KING!

king of the Jews and he had murdered anyone who tried to take his throne, including members of his own family!

The star-watchers had no way of knowing this. They were not Jews themselves. They were from another country far away, east of JERUSALEM, because God wanted everyone to know about Jesus, to bless the whole **WORLD**, just as he had always promised. King Herod

 sent the star-watchers away, and immediately gathered

every PRIEST and SCRIBE and EXPERT he could find.

He asked them only one question: "Where did the holy books say God's long-

promised Messiah would be born?" "In Bethlehem of Judea," they answered.

"For the prophet Micah says that, even though it's just a **LITTLE** town,

out of Bethlehem will come one who will be a ruler and a shepherd of his

people." When his question had been answered, King Herod arranged a secret

meeting with the star-watchers. He asked them how long ago they had first

seen the star and from that information he figured out how old the

child might be. Only then did he REVEAL to them what the priests had

told him about Bethlehem.

"Search for the child," he told them. "And

when you have found him, come back and

tell me EXACTLY where he is, because

I want to worship him too!" That was a LIE. King Herod only wanted to find the child so he could **KILL** him. The star-watchers didn't know

that, though, so off they went, following the star

to Bethlehem. And when it stopped and rested above a

house, they knew they'd found the place. Jesus was no longer a **TINY**,

newborn baby. No, he was a little toddler, living with Mary and Joseph in

that house. And when the star-watchers entered the house, they **FELL** on

their knees before him and worshiped him. Then they gave him precious

gifts—**GOLD** and FRANKINCENSE and **MYRRH**—

gifts fit for a king! When their visit

was finished, did they return to

King Herod and tell him where the

baby was? No, they did not! That's

because God spoke to them in a {DREAM} that told them about the king's

WICKED plan. So in the morning, avoiding the palace, they returned

home another way.

CAN YOU THINK OF ANY OTHER TIMES IN THE BIBLE WHEN GOD HAS SPOKEN IN A DREAM?

JOHN PREPARES THE WAY

John the Baptist had an **AMAZING** story. Do you remember when the

HELLO AGAIN! angel told Mary that her cousin Elizabeth was going to

have a baby? She was old, **REMEMBER?** Well, the baby

she had was JOHN. So he was Jesus's cousin! In fact, the angel

Gabriel had visited John's father, **ZECHARIAH**, and *YUM!*

told him that John would be the one to prepare the way for

Jesus—to let people know that the **SPECIAL**

person God had promised to send was coming and they

should get ready to meet him. And when he grew up, that's

exactly what John did. He lived out in the wild, near the

Jordan River. He wore camel-skin clothes and dined on HONEY

and LOCUSTS! Amazing! And when he talked, people listened.

"Get ready!" he shouted. "God's kingdom is coming. So you need to be

baptized and tell him you are sorry for the wrong things you've done.

MORE than that, you need to **LIVE** differently—in the way God has always wanted you to live." "How?" the people asked him. "If you have more clothes than you need," John replied, "or more food than you can eat, **SHARE** it with someone who doesn't have enough."

I DO HAVE A LOT OF SHIRTS!

"What about us?" some tax collectors asked. "Don't force people to pay more than they owe," John said. "And us?" asked some soldiers. "Be satisfied with what you get paid," said John. "And don't **ACCUSE** people of things they didn't do just so you can SQUEEZE money out of them." When some religious leaders came to see him, men who

HOW RUDE!

thought they were already living the way they should, John had even harsher words for them. "You're **SNAKES**, that's what you are! You think that just because you're part of Abraham's family you don't have to change your ways. WRONG! God could make children of Abraham from these stones if he wanted to. No, you need to change your ways as well!" AMAZING!

Some people thought John was the Messiah, but John corrected them. "No," he explained. "I am the one the **PROPHET** Isaiah told you would come. The voice in the wilderness shouting, 'Prepare the way.' I'm not worthy to untie the sandals of the one who is coming. All I BAPTIZE you with is water, but he will baptize you with God's Holy Spirit and with fire." Then, one day, Jesus came to visit. And John knew **EXACTLY** who he was—God's promised one! "Will you baptize me?" Jesus asked. "Me, baptize you?" John exclaimed. "I think *you* should baptize

me!" "No," said Jesus. "This is right. This is what God wants." So John baptized

JESUS, and when Jesus came up out of the water,

heaven opened and God's Spirit, like a **DOVE**, rested

on him. Then a voice came from heaven. A voice that said, "This

is my Son, the one I love. And I am very **PLEASED** with him!"

  A VERY DEVILISH COMPANION

Jesus was hungry. Not "I need a snack" hungry. Not "I MISSED my lunch and can't wait for dinner" **HUNGRY**. No, Jesus was "I haven't eaten for days and nights" hungry. And that's hungry.

Belly-gnawing, tummy-roaring, finally-and-fully-famished hungry! And why was he hungry? Because God's had led him into the wilderness to FAST. That is, to give up eating so he could focus on getting **CLOSER** to God.

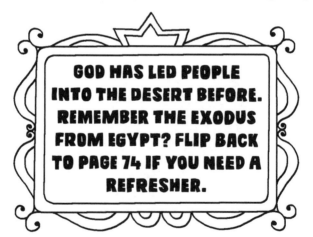

GOD HAS LED PEOPLE INTO THE DESERT BEFORE. REMEMBER THE EXODUS FROM EGYPT? FLIP BACK TO PAGE 74 IF YOU NEED A REFRESHER.

But while he was there, someone else came to meet him. SOMEONE who was

DEFINITELY not God. Someone who was, in fact, the very same "serpent"

who was there from the start—the **DEVIL**. And just as he had tempted

Eve and Adam to disobey God and do what was wrong, he was in the

wilderness to try to do the same thing to Jesus. "So,

you're the Son of God," said the devil, SNAKILY.

Pointing to a pile of rocks, he said, "Well, if that's the case, why not turn

these stones into bread?" Jesus looked at the

devil. He was starving. And he was **TEMPTED** to

do just that. But he was in the desert to get close to God,

so he would always do what God wanted. So this is the

answer he gave: "The SCRIPTURES

say that people need something more

than BREAD to live. They need God's word." "So you trust

God's word, do you?" the devil replied, somehow taking Jesus to the very

top of the temple, far away in Jerusalem. "Well, God's word says that he will

send his angels to **SAVE** his chosen one—to catch him before his foot hits the floor. If you are the Son of God and if you

LOOK AT ALL THOSE KINGDOMS!

trust his word—JUMP!" Jesus looked down, way

down, the hot **WIND** blowing through his hair.

"God's word also says this," he replied. "You shall not put

the Lord your God to the test." "A kingdom!" the devil replied, as

the two of them suddenly stood at the top of a **MOUNTAIN**.

A mountain so **HIGH** that he could see the power and

the riches of every kingdom in the world. "You're here to announce

the arrival of God's kingdom, aren't you? Well, I will give you kingdoms—

every SINGLE kingdom that you see—if you will worship me instead."

Jesus replied, "Again, there are the Scriptures. For God's word says that

we should **WORSHIP** him, and only **SERVE** him. So go away, Satan.

WHAT A TEST FOR JESUS! Leave me alone." And so the devil left. Which

meant Jesus did not give in to those **3** temptations.

Then the ANGELS came to care for God's chosen one.

THE HOMEBOY IS BACK!

Jesus was visiting NAZARETH. It was the town where his mother,

Mary, met the angel Gabriel. The town where her husband, Joseph, worked

as a builder. And it was Jesus's hometown, where he grew

up. Because it was a Saturday, the SABBATH, the day

when Jewish people like Jesus worshiped God, he

went to the SYNAGOGUE. It's what he always did. It was his custom,

his habit, his tradition. And because he was a hometown boy and he was by

now a rabbi—a religious teacher—he was given a

scroll and asked to read a passage from one of

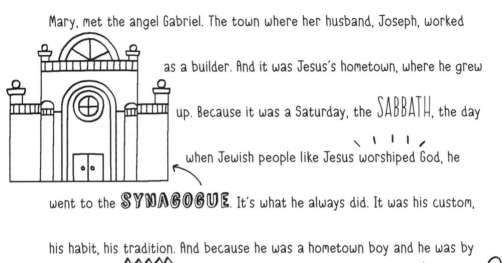

the prophets. Isaiah, as it happens. Remember him? So

Jesus unrolled the scroll and the passage he read went something like this:

"God has given me his **SPIRIT** because he has chosen me to do some very

SPECIAL things: to proclaim good NEWS to the poor,

freedom to the slave, sight to the blind, and rescue and relief to everyone who is knocked 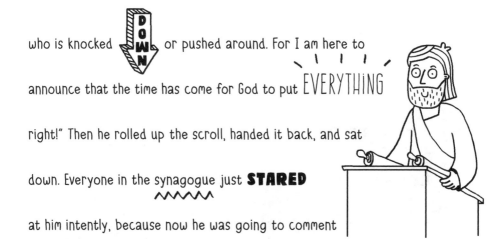 or pushed around. For I am here to

announce that the time has come for God to put EVERYTHING

right!" Then he rolled up the scroll, handed it back, and sat

down. Everyone in the synagogue just **STARED**

at him intently, because now he was going to comment

on what he had read. And they couldn't wait to hear what their hometown

boy had to say. "Today," Jesus said, "these words of Isaiah are coming TRUE.

Right now. Here. Among you!" As he spoke and as he taught, they were all

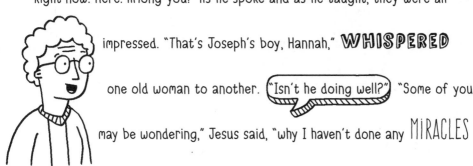 impressed. "That's Joseph's boy, Hannah," WHISPERED

one old woman to another. "Isn't he doing well?" "Some of you

may be wondering," Jesus said, "why I haven't done any MIRACLES

here in my hometown like I did in **CAPERNAUM**. Well, the fact of the

matter is that prophets aren't usually welcome in their hometown. Take

Elijah the prophet, for example. There was no rain in Israel for 3

years and 6 months. And a GREAT famine followed. I'm sure you remember the story. There were surely plenty of **HUNGRY** widows in

his homeland when that famine came. But Elijah was sent by God to provide

 **FOOD** to a widow in Zarephath, a foreigner from a

foreign town. And what about the prophet Elisha? There

were surely plenty of people in Israel, in his homeland, diseased with

LEPROSY. But God helped him to cure the foreigner,

> **WHAT ABOUT US?!**

Naaman, from Syria." As Jesus said this, suddenly the crowd was no

longer impressed with his **TEACHING**. "What's he saying, Hannah?"

whispered one old woman to another. "That God likes those FOREIGNERS

better than his own people? Don't think I like the sound of that!" And neither

did anyone else.  **FURIOUS**, the crowd grabbed

DANGER! LONG WAY DOWN

hold of Jesus and dragged him to a cliffside at the edge

of town. They meant to throw him over that cliff.

But somehow he managed to ESCAPE. And the hometown

boy got away from his hometown as quickly as he could!

A REALLY
TASTY STORY
UP NEXT!

A GREAT CATCH OF FISH

Jesus was by the water, at the Sea of

GALILEE. And the people were EVERYWHERE,

crowding up against the sea to see him! And what

did Jesus see? He saw **2** fishing boats,

with no **FISHERMEN** in them, because they were

washing their nets on the shore. "I see your boats

are free," he said to SIMON, who owned one of the

boats. "Could I borrow yours for a bit?" Simon agreed, and both he and Jesus

climbed (aboard). Simon rowed out a **LITTLE**

way. And from that floating podium,

Jesus talked to the crowd. He told

them all about God's kingdom

and how they should **LOVE**

God and **LOVE** one another,

HOPE HE'S NOT SEASICK!

if God was TRULY in charge of their lives. When the

SOMETHING FISHY'S GOING ON HERE...

talking was done, Jesus said to Simon, "Let's go out into the

deeper water and see if we can catch some fish."

"We were fishing all night," Simon said, "and we

didn't catch a thing. But hey, if you say so, we'll

try again!" So out into the **DEEP** they went.

DOWN into the deep Simon lowered his net. And from somewhere, far, far down,

there was a **TWITCH**. And then a TWIST. And then an **ALMIGHTY**

JAMES

JOHN

TUG that nearly tore the net in two! Up

from the deep Simon tried to pull that net,

but it was so full of fish that he couldn't

do it. So he called out to his fishermen

partners, **JAMES** and **JOHN**, the sons of

Zebedee. With their help, he managed to haul that catch of fish into their

boats and his—such a haul that it THREATENED to sink both

THAT'S A LOT OF FISH!

boats and send them down to the bottom of the deep! Simon was AMAZED, **ASTONISHED**, and OVERWHELMED by what he'd just seen. So he fell on his knees before Jesus. "Go away from me, Lord!" he cried. "I have done many wrong things with my life and don't deserve to be near someone like you!" "Don't be afraid," Jesus told him. "I have a NEW job for you. You will no longer be catching fish, Simon. No, from now on you will be catching people!" When they had all returned to shore, Simon, James, and John left EVERYTHING behind—their boats, their nets, and, yes, that GREAT catch of fish—and went to FOLLOW Jesus.

LIVING IN GOD'S KINGDOM

What does the kingdom of God look like? How do people live when they let

God reign over their lives? Jesus had a lot of SURPRISING things to say

about that. Many of them are gathered in Matthew chapters 5 to 7,

in what people sometimes call (the Sermon on the Mount).

Living in God's kingdom is first of all about being close to God.

So Jesus says that when we are **POOR**, bullied, or sad,

and when we are **MEEK** or desperate to do the right thing,

we are blessed by God—because we are OPEN for him to come

close and go to work in our lives. And when we choose to do

what he would do—when we show mercy, live in a **PURE** way, and try to

make peace—then we are also (blessed) by him, because he is there with us

to help us make those things happen. Even when people try to hurt us or

(STOP) us when we're determined to do what's right, GOD

is there beside us! Living in God's kingdom is also about being an example to others. Jesus says that when we let God reign in our lives, we are

like **SALT**, bringing something TASTY to the world. We're like

a city on a hill, demonstrating God's beauty for all to see. We're

like a **CANDLE**, shining light into darkness. Living in God's

kingdom is about letting God change our hearts too. Hurting

people, calling them names, and even murder don't start with the

action. No, they begin in our hearts when we nurture anger and

bad feelings toward someone. The same is true of being

unfaithful to the people we have married. Much like King David

discovered—REMEMBER what happened between him OOPS!

and Bathsheba?—all it takes sometimes is having a **CRUSH**

on someone when we shouldn't like them that way. As for how

to respond when someone **HURTS** us, living in God's kingdom means

choosing to take control of a situation by not hurting that person back.

It's EASY to love our friends. But living in God's kingdom means loving our **ENEMIES** too! It also means doing  things

quietly and not using them to show off so people see how good we are.

 Praying, giving **MONEY** to the poor, and fasting (not

eating for a while to get close to God) is between us

and him. Nobody else needs to know. Living in God's kingdom means trusting

God to give us what we need to live as well. He doesn't want us to make

what we own the most IMPORTANT thing in our lives. It's here **TODAY**;

gone **TOMORROW**. It doesn't last. So it's not worth putting our trust in

or building our lives around. God doesn't want us to **WORRY** about how

much we have. He's our King and he wants us to trust him to take care of

us. Living in God's kingdom also means not spending our time judging people

when they get things WRONG. It's about looking after our own behavior.

It's about trusting God not only as King but as Father, and asking him

for what we need. It's about treating other people the way we would like

to be treated. It's about listening for the **TRUTH** from people who speak to us and recognizing that there are people who can and will lead us in the

WRONG WAY **WRONG** direction, if we let them. Finally, it's about putting the words of Jesus into ACTION. For then and only then will we have a **STRONG** foundation for our lives and be like a man who has built his house on a rock so it stays strong and doesn't fall apart!

SQUISHINGLY, SQUASHINGLY FULL

Jesus was in the house, teaching. "Love God with all you are!" he said. "And

love your NEIGHBOR as yourself." Jesus was in the house, healing. Healing

the **SICK**, the **BLIND**, and the DEAF. And the house was crowded, really

IT'S REALLY
FULL IN THERE!

crowded. Toe-crunching, body-crushing crowded. Why? Because Pharisees

and teachers of the law from every village in **GALILEE** and every village in

JUDEA, and from the city of Jerusalem, had come to hear him. And that was

a *lot* of teachers and Pharisees! Now, in that town, there were some men

with a friend who was paralyzed. And when they heard that Jesus was

HEALING people, they loaded their friend onto a bed and carried him

to the house. But when they arrived, they **DISCOVERED** that the house was

full. **SQUISHINGLY, SQUASHINGLY**, "no space to sit or squeeze" full.

There was no way those men were going to

WIGGLE or **WAGGLE** or work their

paralyzed friend into that house.

So they did the next best thing.

They carried him up onto the roof—

fortunately it was a <u>flat</u> roof—and they

began to (tear) up the tiles. And when they had torn a hole big enough

for a bed to drop through, they lowered their friend into the house.

SQUASHED and **SQUEEZED**, CROWDED and CRUSHED

as it was, everyone in the house still managed to move out of the way so

the man in the bed would not **DROP** onto their heads.

When Jesus saw the paralyzed man, he spoke to him. But what Jesus said was not what the paralyzed man or his friends expected to hear. "Man," Jesus said, "your sins are forgiven." As it happens, this wasn't what the Pharisees and the teachers of the law **EXPECTED** to hear either. "Who does this Jesus think he is," they thought, "to say such an **OUTRAGEOUS** thing? Only God can forgive sins!" Jesus knew what they were thinking. "What is easier?" he asked them. "To FORGIVE a paralyzed man's sins or tell him to get up and walk? To show you that God himself has given me the right to do the first thing, I will do the second." Then he turned to the paralyzed man. "Get UP and walk!" said Jesus. **SIMPLE** as that. And that's exactly

what the man did! He got up. He picked up his bed.

And he walked right through that crowd. And now the

house wasn't just CRUSHED and CROWDED,

SQUASHED and **SQUEEZED**, filled up full with

people. No, it was filled with praise as well, as one

and all gave thanks to God for the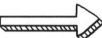

thing they had seen. Jesus was just getting started, though. And there was

more, so much MORE to come...

JESUS'S (INCONVENIENT) NAP TIME

The sun was setting. The day was ending. So Jesus said to his disciples,

"Let's go **ACROSS** to the other side of the lake." They all clambered into

a boat. And with the fading orange sunlight BOUNCING off the water, they

rippled along with the little waves, quiet and calm and peaceful. So peaceful,

in fact, that Jesus fell asleep, his head on a cushion in the back of

the boat. He didn't notice when the dark clouds rolled across the sun.

He didn't notice when the wind **WHIPPED** the little waves into a frenzy.

He didn't notice when those waves washed up into the boat and threatened to drag it to the BOTTOM of the lake. But his disciples noticed. They were **TERRIFIED**, in fact. They shook him and they shouted, "Master! Master! We're going to die! Don't you care?" Of course Jesus cared. And because he was there with his Father and the Spirit when they gathered the **SEAS** together in the first place, and because he was with them when they *BLEW* the first wind into being, there was something he could do as well. "**PEACE**,"

he said. "**QUIET**," he said. And like scolded children, both wind and sea

settled down at his command. And everything was calm. "Why were you

afraid?" he asked his disciples. "After all you've seen, do you not yet

TRUST me?" And, while they were no longer afraid of drowning, the

disciples still felt a shiver, like a wave,

run up and down their spines. "Who

is he," they whispered to one another, "that even the **WIND** and

WAVES obey him?" But there was more, so much more to come...

HOW DID HE DO THAT?

BEATS ME!

FIVE THOUSAND AND MORE HUNGRY TUMMIES

Jesus went across the sea. Then up a mountain too. And people followed,

THOUSANDS and **THOUSANDS** of them. Jesus was

making sick people well to show them

exactly who he was. **EVERYONE**

wanted their sick family members

and friends to be TOUCHED by his healing hands. Finally, Jesus sat down.

And when he looked back over the mountainside, what he saw were those

people—**THOUSANDS** and **THOUSANDS** of them—climbing

up that mountain after him. So he turned to **PHILIP**, one of his disciples,

and said, "These people are hungry. Where do we buy enough bread to feed

them?" They were up a mountain. They were in the middle of NOWHERE.

Jesus knew that. He also knew exactly how he was going to

solve the problem. But he wanted to see how his

disciples would react. And as far as Philip was concerned,

the job seemed **IMPOSSIBLE**. "Even if we spent half a year's salary,"

sighed Philip, "we could only buy enough food to give each

person here a tiny bite." But ANDREW, one of Jesus's other

disciples, had a different answer. "There's a boy here," he said.

"He has **2** fish and **5** loaves of barley bread.

It's not nearly enough to feed everyone ..." But why

mention the **BOY** at all if Andrew didn't think Jesus just might be able to

do something with that little lunch? So Jesus

did. "Tell everyone to sit down," he said.

Down they dropped, five thousand

BOTTOMS and more on the

grassy mountainside. Then Jesus

picked up the FISH and he picked up the BREAD and he thanked God for

them. And when he started breaking them into pieces, the pieces just kept

coming. He gave the pieces to his disciples and his disciples PASSED the

 NO MORE HUNGRY BELLIES! pieces around the crowd. And EVERYONE

ate until there were 5000 and

more full tummies there on that grassy mountainside.

And, yes, there were LEFTOVERS too. That's right, leftovers! "Gather

them up," said Jesus to his disciples. "We don't want to waste one morsel."

Twelve BASKETS full—that's how much they collected. And the people, those

THOUSANDS and THOUSANDS of people, saw something that surpassed

even the healings they had come for. 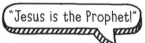 "Jesus is the Prophet!" they shouted.

"The one God promised to send us!" And they would have made him their KING,

 WHERE DID HE GO?! right then and there, if Jesus had not

slipped away.  DUNNO!

GOD'S UNLIMITED FORGIVENESS

Jesus healed people. Lots of people! He **TAUGHT** them too. He was a

RABBI, after all. A Jewish teacher. And what he taught

them about was the kingdom of God. "The kingdom of God

is near..." he would say. "The kingdom of HEAVEN is like..."

he would begin. Then he would go on to explain. Jesus's clearest,

shortest explanation of the kingdom of God was in a prayer he taught his

disciples that is sometimes called "the Lord's Prayer." "Your kingdom

come," Jesus PRAYED to God. "So the things you want to happen on

EARTH really do happen, just like they happen in heaven."

The kingdom of God, then, is when God gets what he wants!

When he actually is King over what people believe is true and how they

act toward him and toward one another. "Love God with **EVERYTHING**

you are," Jesus also said, "and LOVE your neighbor as you love

"HOW MANY TIMES?"

yourself." But what does it look like when God rules?

When he gets what he wants on earth as well as in heaven?

Jesus explained that too. Quite often, he did it by telling

special stories called PARABLES. Like this one: **PETER**, one

of Jesus's disciples, came to him one day with a question: "How often should

I forgive someone who has hurt me?" Then he offered his own answer, which

sounded quite generous. "**SEVEN** times, maybe?" "No,"

Jesus replied. "More like **SEVENTY TIMES SEVEN!**"

Which was more or less Jesus's way of saying, "As many

times as is necessary." Or maybe, by exaggerating the EQUATION, Jesus was

suggesting that forgiveness wasn't about numbers at all but something

much deeper altogether. In any case, what he said was: "This is what the

kingdom of heaven is like..." Then he told Peter a STORY. "Once there

was a man who owed his king some money. Not a little

money. Not a lot of money. But a HUGE, ENORMOUS,

70 X 7 = A LOT

197

GIGANTIC amount of money. Money he could

never, ever afford to pay back. So the king

I FORGIVE YOU!

demanded that the man give him **EVERYTHING** he owned.

And what's more, the king decided to sell the man, his wife, and

his children into SLAVERY! The man fell to his knees and **BEGGED** for

mercy. And guess what? The king felt so sorry for that, he FORGAVE

his debt. Every single penny! Then he sent him on his way, amazed. As the

man left, he ran into another man. A man who owed *him* money. Not a HUGE,

ENORMOUS, GIGANTIC amount of money. Not a lot of money, either.

WHERE'S MY MONEY?

Just a **LITTLE** money. The first man (grabbed) the second man

by the throat. "Pay me what you owe me!" he shouted.

"Be patient, please!" the second man begged. "I'll

pay you back, I promise." But the first man wouldn't

listen. He had the second man thrown into PRISON

until he could pay the debt. There were some other

men watching this. They went to the king and told him what had happened.

When the king heard, he sent for the first man. "You **WICKED** servant!" the king shouted. "You begged for mercy and I forgave everything you owed me. Then you turned around and showed no MERCY whatsoever to a man who owed *you* money. Surely you should have shown your **FELLOW** servant the same mercy I showed you!" With that, the king had the first man thrown into **JAIL** until he could repay his debt. "And that," said Jesus to Peter, "is how your Father in heaven will treat you unless you **TRULY** forgive the person who has hurt you, once and for all, from your heart"

199

AN UNEXPECTED HELPER

A man who was an **EXPERT** in the Jewish law—the rules God had given his people to live by—came to Jesus one day with a question.

I'LL PUT HIM TO THE TEST

The man wanted to TEST Jesus, to see if what Jesus taught was right (or at least what the expert thought was right!). "What do I need to do to **LIVE** with God forever, even after I die?" the expert asked.

So Jesus did what he often did in those situations. He asked the man a

QUESTION in return: "What does the law say? How would you answer that question?" "Love God with **EVERYTHING** you've got," the man replied. "Your HEART and SOUL and STRENGTH and MIND. And love your neighbor as yourself." "Sounds good to me!" said Jesus. And that should have been that. But the expert wanted to show how CLEVER he was. So he asked another question: "Who exactly is my neighbor, then?" And Jesus told him a story.

JESUS'S STORIES

"There was a man **walking** along the road from Jerusalem to Jericho.

Suddenly, a gang of **ROBBERS** grabbed him and beat him, stole his

CLOTHES, and left him for dead. A little while later, a **PRIEST** came by.

And when he saw the man, he (crossed) over to the other side of the road

and just left him there. A short while later, a man who served God in the

TEMPLE came by. And when he saw the man, he

also crossed over to the other side of the road

and left him there. Who should come by next but a

SAMARITAN. That's right, the Jewish people's sworn enemy. Unlike the first two men, the Samaritan

OH NO! HE NEEDS MY HELP!

HERE TO HELP!

felt **SORRY** for that poor, beaten stranger by the road. He bent down and bandaged up the man's wounds. He picked him up and placed him on his DONKEY. Then he took him to a nearby inn. And when he went on his way, he gave the innkeeper coins worth a couple of days' **WAGES** and a set of instructions. "Take care of this man," he said. "If this doesn't cover the cost, I'll pay you the rest when I return." Then Jesus looked at the expert and asked one more QUESTION: "Which of these 3 proved himself to be a **NEIGHBOR** to the wounded man?" "The one who showed him mercy," the expert replied. "Then GO! and do the same!" said Jesus. And that was the **END** of the man's questions.

HE REALLY IS CLEVER!

 # LOST PROPERTY

OINK!

 PHARISEES were religious leaders who tried their **BEST** to follow the

Jewish laws—the **RULES** for living that God had given to Moses. That

helped them to do some very good things. But it also sometimes

made them proud, so they looked **DOWN** on people who weren't

trying as HARD as they were. As a result, the Pharisees were

annoyed and confused when they saw Jesus spending time with people

who had done lots of bad things. So Jesus told them **3** stories with

pretty much the same meaning. The reason for three was so they wouldn't

miss the point that the kingdom of God is about finding the lost,

FORGIVENESS, and second chances. The first story was about a

WHERE IS IT? SHEPHERD who had **100** sheep. One of them

wandered away. So he left his other ninety-nine

sheep and went to look for the OVER HERE!

LOST one. When he found it, he carried

it home. Then he threw a **PARTY** to celebrate the sheep's return. "In the same way," Jesus told the Pharisees, "there is more CELEBRATION in heaven over one **SINNER** who turns away from what is wrong and returns to God than over ninety-nine people who don't need to turn back to him." The second story was about a woman who lost one of her 10 coins. She lit a lamp, swept her house, and searched persistently until she found it. When she did, just like the shepherd, she threw a **PARTY**. "The angels celebrate too," said Jesus, "when even one person changes their ways and turns back to God." The third story was about a man with 2 sons. The younger son **DESPERATELY** wanted to leave home. So he asked his father for the money he would receive

OFF I GO! as an INHERITANCE when the old man died. The father gave him the money and off he went to a far, far country. In no time at all, the **MONEY** was spent, foolishly, on **BAD** things. And as soon as it was gone, a famine struck, and

the younger son was hungry. The only job he could find was feeding PIGS.

Now he was **DESPERATE** again—this time

FEED ME!

to eat the pigs' food. That's when, as Jesus put it, the

younger son "came to his senses." He realized that even

his father's **SERVANTS** were better off than he was. So he decided to

return home, admit that he'd been wrong, and apologize to his father for

what he'd done. He was (convinced) he was no longer worthy to be called

his father's son and hoped his dad would hire him as a servant. As the

LOOKING SHARP!

son neared home, though, his father came RUNNING

to meet him! His father **HUGGED** him and kissed

him, and when the son asked to be made

a servant, the father refused. He called for a

ROBE, a RING, and a fresh pair of SHOES for the

young man. "Kill the best calf we have," he told his

servants, "and cook it up. My son is back! So let's celebrate!"

The older brother wasn't in a **CELEBRATING** mood, however. Much like the Pharisees, he couldn't understand why his father was throwing a party for someone who'd done so much **WRONG**. "He went away and wasted your money!" the older son complained. "But I've been here, **FAITHFULLY** serving you, and you've never thrown even one party for me!" "Don't you see?" the father replied. "You've had me and all that was mine for all these years. But your brother was gone and now he's back. He was dead and now he's ALIVE. He was lost and now he's found. What can we do except celebrate?"

ANOTHER AMAZING STORY NEXT!

WHAT AN ENTRANCE!

Jesus was on his way to **JERUSALEM**. When he came close to the Mount of

Olives that stood above the city, he pulled two of his disciples to one side

and gave them the following INSTRUCTIONS: "There's a village UP ahead.

UNTIE THIS DONKEY!

In the village you will find a young donkey. A

donkey that has never been ridden. Untie

the donkey and bring it to me." The disciples looked

PUZZLED. Who wouldn't? Steal a donkey for Jesus?

It just didn't sound right. "If the owner asks you why

you are UNTYING his donkey," Jesus went on, "tell him the Lord needs it."

So into the village the two disciples went. Up to the **DONKEY** the two

disciples walked. And, using their best knot-untying skills, they released the

OK THEN! donkey. When the donkey's owner asked

them what they were doing, they simply replied, "The Lord

needs it." Maybe the owner was INCREDIBLY relaxed about his

donkey. Maybe the owner was in the donkey-hiring business and the donkey had been **RESERVED** for this occasion. Or maybe the words were a code that the owner had an **AGREEMENT** with Jesus. For whatever reason, the owner let the two disciples take the young donkey back to Jesus. Then the disciples draped their CLOAKS over the donkey and put Jesus on its back. And into Jerusalem he rode. Some of the disciples spread more cloaks on the road ahead of him. Some people cut palm **BRANCHES** from trees and **SPREAD** those in the road as well. And, together, that crowd SHOUTED, "Blessed is the

KING who comes in God's name! Peace in heaven! Glory in the highest!

HOSANNA, save us, Son of David!" But there were some Pharisees who

were not pleased by this **"PARADE"** at all. It looked to them as if the

people thought Jesus was God's LONG-PROMISED savior, the Messiah.

"Tell your disciples to be quiet!" the Pharisees Shhh

said to Jesus. "Be quiet?" Jesus replied.

PRAISE TO JESUS!

"Don't be **RIDICULOUS!** Even if my followers

fell silent, the stones they

stand on would cry out in praise!"

A HOUSE OF THIEVES

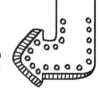

Jesus followed his long donkey ride  **DOWN** into

Jerusalem with a visit to the temple. And when he

looked around, he wasn't very **HAPPY** with

what he saw. First, there were the **MONEY**

CHANGERS. Their job was simple. And profitable. And not particularly

fair. People had to use a special temple COIN to pay a special temple tax.

So they had to exchange their regular money for those

SPECIAL coins. And the money changers

WHAT A
MONEY-
MAKER!

took advantage of that by

charging more than they should for

those special coins. That made Jesus **ANGRY**. So did the price the

DOVE SELLERS were charging for their doves.

HOW
MUCH?!

Poor people, and poor women in particular,

couldn't afford a bigger animal to sacrifice

at the temple. So they **BOUGHT** doves. And, yes, much like the money

changers, the dove sellers took **ADVANTAGE** of that to charge more

than they should. So what did Jesus do? He OVERTURNED the tables of

the money changers so their coins went

CLATTERING up and down the

temple courtyard. He knocked over the

seats of the dove sellers too! "My

house should be a house of prayer!" he

shouted. "That's what our **SCRIPTURES**

say. But you people have turned it into a house of thieves!" Then, to show

the difference, Jesus turned the temple back into a house of PRAYER

again. He healed people who couldn't see and people who couldn't

walk. And, when they saw it, children began to shout, "**HOSANNA!**

Thank you for saving us, Son of David!"

HOSANNA!

HOSANNA!

PRAISE JESUS!

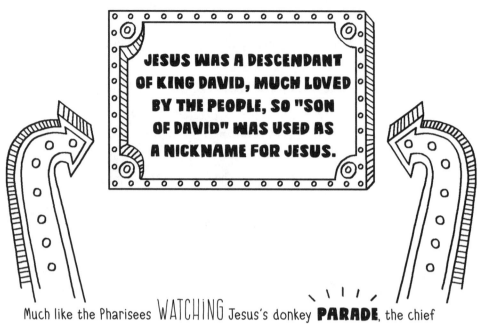

JESUS WAS A DESCENDANT OF KING DAVID, MUCH LOVED BY THE PEOPLE, SO "SON OF DAVID" WAS USED AS A NICKNAME FOR JESUS.

Much like the Pharisees WATCHING Jesus's donkey **PARADE**, the chief priests and the scribes were not happy with this at all. Because it

WHAT'S HE SAYING?!

sounded as if the children were claiming that Jesus was God's **LONG-PROMISED** savior, the Messiah. "Do you hear what they are saying?" the priests COMPLAINED to Jesus. "I do," Jesus replied. "Have you never read what our **SCRIPTURES** say? 'Even from the mouths

IT SAYS IT RIGHT THERE!

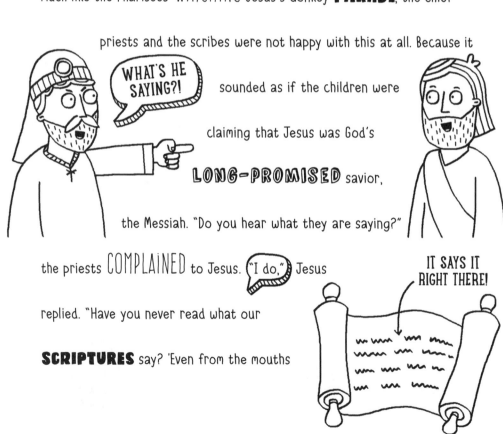

of infants and babies, God receives PRAISE!'" Then he left them and went

to stay with friends in a village called Bethany.

A SAD STORY UP NEXT!

A NIGHT OF SURPRISES

Jesus was in Jerusalem. He was there to CELEBRATE the Passover feast, to REMEMBER how God had spared everyone whose house was marked with the blood of an innocent lamb.

GO BACK AND LOOK!

DO YOU REMEMBER THIS STORY? IT'S SERIOUSLY EPIC—TURN BACK TO PAGE 70 IF YOU WANT TO REREAD IT!

He knew that he was about to die, just like that lamb. He even knew that his disciple, **JUDAS**, had agreed to BETRAY him to his enemies. So he arranged a place to eat. And he gathered with his disciples to share a meal. Then SURPRISE! he did something that no one else in the room expected. He took off his robe, tied a towel around his waist, filled a basin with water, and began to wash his disciples' feet.

SIMON PETER spoke up, like he always did. "Do you mean to wash my feet?" he asked. "I do," Jesus replied. "And one day you will UNDERSTAND why." "No!" insisted Peter, shaking his head. "You will never wash my feet!"

Now perhaps Peter's feet were particularly **SMELLY** that day. More likely, he knew this was a servant's job and not

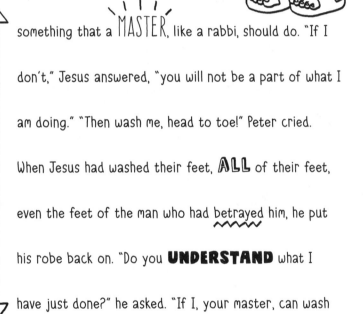

something that a MASTER, like a rabbi, should do. "If I don't," Jesus answered, "you will not be a part of what I am doing." "Then wash me, head to toe!" Peter cried.

When Jesus had washed their feet, **ALL** of their feet, even the feet of the man who had betrayed him, he put his robe back on. "Do you **UNDERSTAND** what I have just done?" he asked. "If I, your master, can wash

your feet, then surely you can wash each other's feet. For a servant is not **GREATER** than his master. Know this. And more than that, do it. Serve one another!" Then Jesus looked sad. He had

another **SURPRISE** in store for them. A surprise that was not very nice.

"One of you will betray me," he sighed. The surprise worked. The disciples

couldn't **BELIEVE** it and spent the next few minutes CHATTERING,

CONFUSED, among themselves. "Who? Who is it?" they wanted

to know. So Jesus dipped a piece of bread into some

sauce. "The one I give this to," he said, "is my betrayer." And

he handed the bread to **JUDAS**. "Do what you have to do,"

he whispered to Judas. "And do it quickly." When Judas had gone, Jesus

took another piece of bread. There was one last surprising thing he

needed to do. He THANKED God for the bread. Then he passed it around

to his disciples and said, "Eat this; it's my body." When they had done so, he **PICKED** up a cup of wine and thanked God for that as well.

"Drink this," he told them. "It's my BLOOD. God made promises

to his people in the past, to **ABRAHAM** and to

MOSES and to **DAVID**. This is his new promise,

a promise of forgiveness made possible through my blood.

And, listen, I will not drink from this cup with you again until I am made

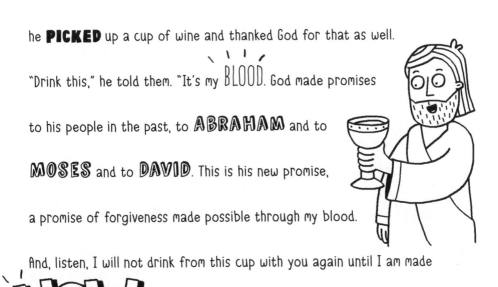

in the kingdom of my Father." When the meal was

finished, Jesus and his disciples **SANG** a hymn and then

WALKED toward the Mount of Olives. Only Jesus knew that

a night of sad surprises lay before them.

WHAT COULD THE SAD SURPRISE BE?

A VERY DARK DAY

The night began with prayer in a garden called **GETHSEMANE**.

Jesus knew that he was going to die, because his enemies wanted him

gone. It was also what God wanted, and what the

PROPHETS had promised—that the **MESSIAH**

ALL THOSE
SINS! would be a lamb, sacrificed for the

sins of the world. Judas had already

gone to tell Jesus's enemies where he was. They'd

arrive soon. So Jesus prayed. "Take away this cup," he

said, "these **AWFUL** things I must suffer. But if it truly is what you

want, Father, I will do it." Then it began. One awful thing followed

another. First, there was a KISS. Judas planted it on Jesus's cheek

THERE
HE IS!

so the temple guards with their clubs and

swords knew **EXACTLY** which man to

arrest. A religious court came next. Jesus

was dragged before the high priest and the other religious leaders. Witnesses **LIED** about him. When he finally admitted that he was, indeed, the Messiah God had promised to send, they were , and sentenced him to **DEATH**. Then the mocking began. They made fun of him. Spat in his face. They **BLINDFOLDED** him and dared him to say who had hit him. Then they took him to **PILATE**, the Roman governor, and there was a trial. "This man says he's king to rival CAESAR, the Roman emperor," they said to Pilate. "He must die!" But when Pilate questioned Jesus, he couldn't find that he'd done anything wrong. So the religious leaders whipped up the crowd to cry out, "**CRUCIFY HIM!**" Eager to avoid a RIOT, Pilate gave in. "I am  of this man's blood," he announced

PILATE

CRUCIFY JESUS!

as he washed his hands. And he turned Jesus over to his soldiers. Then it was

HORROR on **HORROR**.

A CRIMINAL. That's how those soldiers treated Jesus.

They whipped his back until it bled. Tore off his **CLOTHES** and replaced them with a red robe. They jammed a crown made of THORNS on his head. Stuck a reed in his hand as a pretend scepter. They bowed before him and mocked him. "Hail, King of the Jews!" they cried. Then they tore off the robe and **BEAT** him with the reed and led him away to be crucified. **A WOODEN CROSS**—that's what they laid on his bleeding back.

They marched him to a hill called **THE SKULL** . They laid him on the

 cross; hammered nails through his **HANDS** and **FEET** to

pin him to the wood. Then they raised the cross between two

others for everyone to see. Then there were the **CURSES** from his

enemies. And from a thief on one of those other crosses. "If you're

really the Messiah," the man demanded, "save yourself and us too!"

But the thief hanging on the other side said, "We **DESERVE** to be

here. But this man's done nothing wrong." Then he asked Jesus to take him

to his kingdom when he died. Jesus replied, "Today

you will be with me in **PARADISE**." Jesus's mom

was **CRYING** as she waited there

and watched him SUFFER. So Jesus

asked his disciple John to take her home with him. Even the

soldiers received Jesus's kindness. As they gambled for his clothes, he

asked God to forgive them. Then the sky grew dark.

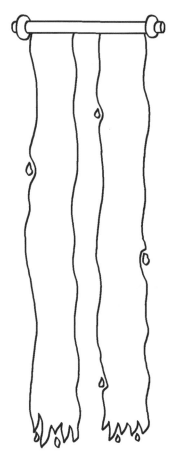

And that's when it happened. The **CURTAIN** in the temple that hung between the people and the most ⟨holy⟩ place—a sign of the distance between them and God—was torn in two. As it tore, Jesus BREATHED his last words: "Into your hands, Father, I commit my spirit." Then a (centurion)—a Roman commander who'd been watching—said, "Surely, this man was **INNOCENT**."

And it was over. All that Jesus's enemies had hoped for. Or so they thought. Because the promise of the prophets and all that God wanted was yet to be revealed. And there was more, so much  to come!

THE GREATEST MIRACLE OF ALL

It was dark. Dark before dawn. And dark in the **hearts** of the women who

crept to the tomb. Their friend Jesus was dead and **SADNESS**

surrounded them like a shadow. But MARY MAGDALENE, JOANNA, and

another MARY, the mother of James, had a job to do. They had to **cover**

Jesus's body with **SPICES**, according to the custom

of that time. It wouldn't be easy to look again at the wounds he had

SUFFERED as he died. But they were determined to do this one last act of

kindness for their friend.

Silently they went and,

as dawn broke, they saw

the **TOMB**. And each

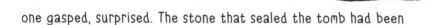

one gasped, surprised. The stone that sealed the tomb had been

ROLLED away! They went inside. There was no body. And their

surprise turned to confusion. Where was he? Who had taken him?

That's when  2 angels appeared, WHITE and BRIGHT and frightening. And the women fell facedown on the ground, confusion replaced by fear. "Why are you looking for your friend here?" the angels asked. "This is a place for DEAD people. But

your friend Jesus is ALIVE! He has risen! Back when you were with him in Galilee, he told you what would happen. REMEMBER? He said that the Messiah would be handed over to evil men and crucified. And would then rise

again in 3 days' time." Of course they

SEE! WE TOLD YOU!

remembered! And as they hurried to tell the rest of Jesus's disciples their GOOD news,

227

it all came flooding back. But when they got there and described what they

had seen, no one (believed) them! The other disciples thought they were

making the **WHOLE** thing up. So off Peter went to see

for himself. When he entered the tomb, he found nothing

but the LINEN cloths in which

Jesus's body had been wrapped.

And, like the women, he went back to the

others, AMAZED. It got them all talking.

Where was Jesus now? Why hadn't they

expected this? Why had they FORGOTTEN what

he'd told them? What would happen next? They

talked about it all day. And then, that evening, **2** of the disciples, who

had gone back to their home in **EMMAUS**, came rushing back with the

news that they had actually SEEN Jesus and talked with him on the

road. That's when Jesus appeared to the rest. Just like that, in the room, out of NOWHERE! The disciples were terrified. They thought he

was a ghost. **BOO!** But Jesus put their minds to rest.

"Ghosts don't have bones," he said. "Touch my **HANDS** and **FEET** and

you'll see. It's me! And, come to think of it, I'm feeling a little hungry."

So they made him a meal. And through a mouthful of fish he added, "Ghosts

don't need to eat, either!"

FINALLY, he talked them

through all the things that

MOSES, the prophets, and the psalms had said would happen to the Messiah.

He helped them to **UNDERSTAND** that God's special promised one was always supposed to die and be resurrected, and that he had come to

turn people's **HEARTS** back to God and forgive them for all the wrong

things they had done. "You are my witnesses," he told

them. "You WATCHED  everything I did, HEARD

everything I taught. And now you see me here, alive ! So go and tell

the world, starting right here in Jerusalem. But don't go just yet, for

I have 1 more **GIFT** to leave with you. The promise of my

Father that will give you the power you need to do what I've asked." Then,

as quickly as he had come, Jesus left.

A GOOD IDEA THIS WAY!

JESUS'S BRIGHT IDEA

Jesus was **ALIVE!** And over the next forty days, he visited his friends,

 in all. One minute he was doing IMPOSSIBLE things, like

appearing out of nowhere in a locked room. The next he was doing ordinary,

everyday things, like cooking fish at the seaside. It was all down to his

brand-new resurrected **BODY**, a body built to last forever. "I want you to

tell my story to everyone, everywhere," Jesus told his disciples. "Make them

disciples too. Baptize them in the name of the **FATHER** and the SON and

the **HOLY SPIRIT**. Teach them everything that I have taught you. And

I will be with you as you do it. Forever. Always."

But how was he going to do that, exactly—be with

them everywhere and always? This is how: First, Jesus told

them to wait in Jerusalem. God had something amazing to

give them. Then, Jesus led them to

the top of a MOUNTAIN. As they

watched, he rose into the sky and disappeared

into a CLOUD. "Don't worry," 2 angels

announced. "He'll come back one day in the

very same way you saw him go." So the

disciples went to JERUSALEM and waited. And, forty days later, as they were

praying in a small room, the promise came! Like so many of God's PROMISES,

it came with WIND and FIRE. Wind that filled the room and fire that burned

above each head. It was the PROMISE of God's Holy Spirit. And when God's

Spirit fell on them, each disciple started to speak in LANGUAGES they had

never learned. Languages of every land. Languages to tell the story of

Jesus. Out into the streets they stumbled, TELLING the story in every nation's tongue. And because it was the Feast of **PENTECOST**, Jews from

every nation were gathered in those streets and wondered, out loud, how

they were HEARING the story in their own language.

"These are uneducated people from little villages and towns up

north in Galilee," the crowd observed. "How are they doing

this?" "They're just babbling!" someone suggested. "They've

had too much to drink!" So Peter addressed the crowd and set

them **STRAIGHT**. "We are not filled with drink!" he explained.

"We are filled with God's Holy Spirit! Many years ago, the prophet **JOEL** said

this would happen—that all people, YOUNG and OLD, MEN and WOMEN,

SLAVES and MASTERS, would receive God's Spirit. And how did this

happen? Because of Jesus, that's how! Jesus, who performed **MIRACLES**

among you. Jesus, who taught you about God's kingdom.

JESUS, who was the Messiah we've all been

waiting for. And Jesus, whom you crucified.

But because he was the MESSIAH, God raised

him from the dead and we have seen him! That's

right, we are witnesses to a living Messiah, who has ascended to God and

now reigns at his side!" The crowds were **SHOCKED** by this news. They had

killed the very one they had been waiting for. So they cried out to Peter,

asking, "What should we do?" "Tell God you're **sorry** for

what you did," Peter replied. "Choose to live differently from now on. Be

baptized in the name of Jesus. Receive God's forgiveness. And this **GIFT**

of God's Holy Spirit will be yours as well!" So that's what the people did,

3,000 of them in all! And this was just the START of a

story that spread from there across the **WORLD**. That's right,

there's more! So much **MORE** to come!

THE NEWEST FAMILY MEMBERS

From a **SMALL** gathering in a small room, the number of people who

followed Jesus had grown by  in just one day! What

were they meant to do? They needed to find out more about Jesus for a

start. So the apostles, the men (apart from Judas, of course)

who had been Jesus's disciples and spent three years with him, passed on

what Jesus had **TAUGHT** them. But there was more. The new followers

of Jesus hung out together, prayed, and ate together. They also celebrated

that **SPECIAL** meal Jesus had shared with his disciples—the bread

for his body and the wine for his blood. They shared their

possessions too. And if anyone needed ANYTHING, someone else would sell something they owned to meet that need! They also **FAITHFULY** went

to the temple. Like Jesus and his disciples, they were Jewish and the temple

was where they WORSHIPED God. As a result, many more people (followed)

Jesus. It helped that the apostles performed some of the same miracles

Jesus did. **MIRACLES** like this one: Peter and John were on their way

to the temple. Sitting outside the temple gate

ANY SPARE COINS?

called **"BEAUTIFUL"** was a man who couldn't

walk. Everyone knew him. He'd been lame from birth and was

carried there EVERY day so he could beg.

When he saw Peter and John, he asked them for money. Peter simply said,

"Look at us." The man took this as a **GOOD** sign. If people

didn't want to give him money, they usually ignored him. So he looked at

Peter, expecting a few coins. But Peter had **SOMETHING**

different in mind. "I don't have any silver or gold," he said, "but I'll give you

what I do have. In the name of JESUS OF NAZARETH, Jesus the Messiah, stand up and walk!" Then Peter took hold of the man's right hand and **RAISED** him to his feet. And, sure enough, the man could walk. In fact, he leaped for **JOY!** When Peter and John entered the temple, the man went with them, WALKING and LEAPING and PRAISING GOD. "Isn't that the lame man who's always begging at the temple gate?" people asked. "How has this happened?" So, much as he had done on the day of **PENTECOST**, Peter answered their questions: "We didn't make this man well. He was **HEALED** through the POWER of Jesus—the long-promised one sent by God. The one you killed and God raised from the DEAD. We saw him alive! It's through our trust in him that this man now walks. You need to say you're **SORRY** for your part in killing him, turn away from your sins, and receive God's forgiveness. And you must accept that he was indeed the Messiah that **BOTH** Moses and the prophets

238

said would one day come." Many in the crowd believed what Peter said. In fact, the number of believers rose to **FIVE THOUSAND**. But some religious leaders didn't like him saying that Jesus had been resurrected from the dead. So Peter and John were ARRESTED and put in jail.

> ALL WE DID WAS HEAL HIM!

"We've done nothing more than heal a man who couldn't walk for 40 years," argued Peter and John. The people were thrilled that the man could walk. What could the religious leaders do? They could hardly PUNISH Peter and John for that. Even when they demanded that Peter and John STOP talking about Jesus, Peter bravely replied that he was **OBLIGED** to follow God, not men. So they were set FREE. The other believers rejoiced. And they kept on telling **MORE** and **MORE** people the good news of Jesus!

FROM BULLY TO BLIND MAN TO BELIEVER

SAUL was a smart man, a good teacher, and passionate about his Jewish faith. The followers of Jesus were **PASSIONATE** about their Jewish faith too. They believed that Jesus was God's Messiah, the savior he had always promised to send. And that's where they had a disagreement with Saul. As far as Saul was concerned, Jesus was **NOT** the Messiah and definitely had not been resurrected from the dead. It was all a LIE that needed to be **STOPPED**. But the more he CHASED the followers of Jesus, the farther they ran. And, much to his dismay, the farther their "false" teaching spread! It had started in Jerusalem, gone to **SAMARIA**, and reports that Saul received suggested it was now up north in the Syrian city of **DAMASCUS**. So he asked for permission to travel to Damascus and ARREST any

followers of Jesus he found there.

He was going to put an end to this once

and for all! God had different plans, though.

God, who is an expert in finding exactly the

"wrong" people to do his will: **NINETY-YEAR-OLDS** to father nations.

Stammering **SHEPHERDS** to confront pharaohs. Boys to kill

GIANTS. That sort of thing. So, as Saul made his way along the

REMEMBER?

road to Damascus, God grabbed his attention. It wasn't quite a burning

bush but it worked just as well. A **BRIGHT** light from heaven shone around

Saul, **BLINDING** him. And, as Saul fell to the ground, a voice from heaven

followed. "Saul," the voice said. "Oh, Saul. Why are you working so hard to do

me harm?" "I don't even know who you are!" Saul cried. "I'm Jesus," the

voice replied. "It's me you're HURTING when you go after my

followers. So get . Get up now. Go into Damascus

and you will be told what you need to do next." So Saul

got up. And since the men who were with him had also heard the **VOICE**, they were more than willing to escort their now-blind **COMPANION** by the hand into the city. For **3** days, Saul waited there in the darkness. He ate nothing. He drank nothing, either. EVERYTHING he believed, EVERYTHING he had fought for, had been turned upside down. Jesus really was **ALIVE**. He had spoken to him. But what would Jesus do now, Saul wondered, to someone who had hunted down ANANIAS

his followers and agreed to their deaths? The answer to that question arrived in the shape of a follower of Jesus called **ANANIAS**. Jesus had spoken to him as well. And even though there was no blinding light, it was every bit as dramatic! "Go to Straight Street," said Jesus. "To the house where Judas

JUDAS'S HOUSE

lives." (This is a different Judas.) "Saul of Tarsus is staying there. He's been praying. And in a **VISION** he has seen a man, who looks

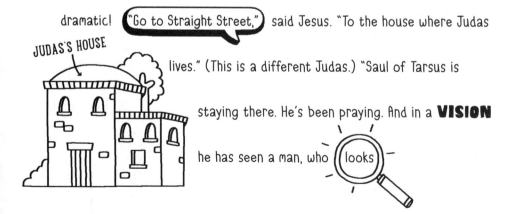

REMARKABLY like you, laying hands

on him so he can see again." "Saul of

Tarsus?" Ananias cried. "Killing-your-

followers Saul? Throwing-us-in-prison Saul? That Saul?" "That

would be the one," Jesus replied. "I have plans for

him, you see. PEOPLE who are not

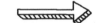

Jewish need to know about me too. And I

have chosen Saul to be the man who tells them!" So Ananias went to Straight

Street, to the house of Judas. When he **FOUND** Saul, he laid his hands

on him. Saul **REGAINED** his sight and was filled with God's Holy Spirit.

And Saul was baptized. And Saul ate. And straight away, Saul went out into

Damascus, not to ARREST the followers of Jesus but to join them and tell

 about him!

EXPANDING THE DINNER MENU

"A blessing to the whole world." That's what God told Abraham his family

would be, **REMEMBER?** Even before Abraham *had* a family! Which meant

that God wasn't interested only in Abraham's family and the

nation that sprang from it but in EVERY other kind of

family in the **WORLD**. People who were Jewish and people who weren't. So

when God told Ananias that he had chosen Saul to tell his story to the

GENTILES, that's what he was up to. "Gentile" was the name

Jewish people gave to those who weren't part of Abraham's family.

But even though Moses had spoken about this, and the prophets

and Jesus too, God still needed to make it ABSOLUTELY clear

to Jesus's followers—to their leaders in particular. One day, while Peter was

praying on the rooftop of a house in **JOPPA**, God gave him a

vision. Peter was **HUNGRY**. Dinner wasn't yet ready

and, while he waited, he fell into a kind of **DREAMING** state; a trance.

The heavens opened and he saw a **LARGE** sheet, let down by its four corners.

The sheet was writhing and squirming, because it was filled with animals, birds,

and reptiles. Through the **SQUAWKING** and HISSING, **CHATTERING**

and SNORTING, Peter heard a voice. "Get up, Peter! Kill and eat!" Now, apart

from the fact that Peter hadn't intended to kill, pluck, and prepare his own

DINNER, there was a problem: every creature in the sheet was on the

list of animals that Jewish people were not **PERMITTED** to eat. Pigs and

pelicans. Ferrets and frogs. Mice and moles. And a WHOLE lot more besides. So

Peter said, "No! I won't! I've never eaten the kind of

'unclean' food that our law tells us we shouldn't eat!" The voice simply replied, "If God calls something '**CLEAN**,' you shouldn't call it 'unclean!'"

Three times this happened. And when the VISION was finished and Peter was trying to work out what it meant, someone called through the gates below.

"We're looking for Peter," the visitors said. "Is he here?" The Holy Spirit told Peter to go **DOWN** and meet them. "I've sent them," the Spirit said. "I want you to go with them." When Peter spoke to the men, the meaning of his vision started to become CLEAR. "We've come from Cornelius, who lives in

CORNELIUS

Caesarea," they explained. "He is a **GOD-FEARING** man, well-thought of by the Jews but he is not a Jew himself. An angel appeared to him in a vision and told him to invite you to his HOUSE. That's why we're here." Jews were not meant to eat "unclean" food. They were not **MEANT** to go into the homes of "unclean" people, either—people like this Gentile, CORNELIUS.

But if God was telling him to go to Cornelius's house,

thought Peter, then, much like the food, it was because God had made

associating with Gentiles a **"CLEAN"** thing to do. So, along with some other

followers of Jesus, Peter went with the men to meet Cornelius. When Peter

arrived at Cornelius's house, it was FILLED with his family and friends, Gentiles

just like him. Peter told everyone there about Jesus. Even before he'd finished

speaking, the **HOLY SPIRIT** fell on those Gentiles just like he'd fallen

on Peter and his friends on the day of Pentecost! They spoke in **TONGUES**.

They PRAISED God. Peter and his Jewish friends were amazed. Peter baptized

everyone in that house and they became followers of Jesus too. Gentiles! No

longer "unclean" like **PIGS** and **PELICANS**, FERRETS and **FROGS**, but

welcome in God's family, just as he had always intended.

WOW!

SHAKING THINGS UP (LITERALLY)

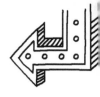

On and on Saul went, telling the story of Jesus while traveling with his friend,

Barnabas. And somewhere along the way, Saul started going by another name:

Paul. **WEEK** by **WEEK**, MONTH by MONTH, **YEAR**

by **YEAR**, and CITY by CITY, he spread the good news

to anyone who would listen. And listen they did! Both **JEWS** and

GENTILES believed what he said and became followers of Jesus too.

So when he left their cities and towns, he left small groups of BELIEVERS

behind—little churches of people who prayed, sang, and encouraged one

another. When that long trip was finally over, Paul and Barnabas returned

to Jerusalem. The apostles there were **EXCITED** to hear how many

people had put their faith in Jesus. But when the time came for a second

SILAS
PAUL
trip, Paul was joined by a man called **SILAS** and

then a younger man called **TIMOTHY**, whom they met in

Lystra. Until now, Paul had only visited cities in

ASIA MINOR (modern-day Turkey). He'd planned to keep telling the story of Jesus around there but the **HOLY SPIRIT** wouldn't let him. Paul saw a vision one night of a man from MACEDONIA (on the edges of what is now Europe) asking him to come that way instead. So Paul and his companions **CROSSED** the waters to Macedonia. The story of Jesus was about to spread even **FARTHER!** They went to a (city) called Philippi. There they met a businesswoman called Lydia. When they told her about Jesus, she and EVERYONE else in her house were baptized. Things were looking good! But then they came across a slave girl who was used by the men who owned her to tell fortunes. Paul realized she could do that because an **EVIL** spirit had taken control of her. So, in the name of Jesus, he made that spirit leave. The girl was **HEALED** but the men who owned

THANK YOU!

249

her were furious because she could no longer make money for them. So they

DRAGGED Paul and Silas before a judge in the marketplace. And the judge

decided that Paul and Silas should be BEATEN and (thrown) into jail.

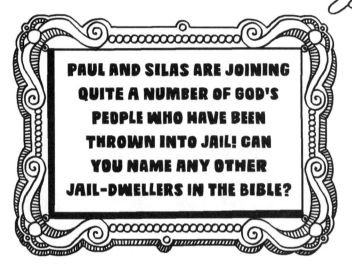

**PAUL AND SILAS ARE JOINING
QUITE A NUMBER OF GOD'S
PEOPLE WHO HAVE BEEN
THROWN INTO JAIL! CAN
YOU NAME ANY OTHER
JAIL-DWELLERS IN THE BIBLE?**

It had all started so well, this trip across the water. But now they

were locked up in prison, their **FEET** fastened tight in wooden stocks.

Did that make Paul and Silas give up? Did it SHATTER their trust in

God? It did not! Deep into the night and **DEEP** in the middle of that

prison, they prayed and **SANG** songs of praise to God. The other

PRISONERS heard them. Singing was another way to tell the story of Jesus.

Then, suddenly,  EVERYTHING started to

SHAKE. Doors flew open, chains fell off, and

Paul and Silas's stocks were unlocked. It was an

EARTHQUAKE! The jailer rushed in. He saw the open doors. Then he drew

his word to kill himself, because he'd be put to death if any prisoner

 escaped. "Stop!" cried Paul from out

of the darkness. "Don't hurt yourself. We're

all still here." The jailer called for a TORCH

and, sure enough, not 1 prisoner had escaped. "What should

I do to be saved?" he asked Silas and Paul, still worried about what might

happen to him. So Paul told him the story he told everyone. "Trust in Jesus,"

he said, "and you and EVERYONE in your house will be saved." The jailer

took Paul and Silas to his home. He washed their wounds. And Paul and Silas

baptized the jailer and his family, and their sins were WASHED away. Then

they all had a meal together. And the story of Jesus just kept spreading.

A NEW HEAVEN AND A NEW EARTH

John was old. Very old. It seemed like a **LIFETIME** and more since he

had left his fishing boat and followed Jesus's call to be one of his disciples.

Three years *RUSHED* by. And he saw so **MUCH** and he learned so much from

Jesus. And when Jesus died, he was the only disciple watching, and he took

his master's mom home to care for her. Then **3** days crawled by. Three

long, **SAD** days. And when the women came to say that Jesus's body was

missing, John *RACED* his friend Peter to the tomb to see for himself. Jesus

was, indeed, gone. But then, later that day, he

wasn't! For he appeared to them all, alive again,

resurrected from the dead. Forty days later, up

into heaven Jesus went. As John and his friends waited

in Jerusalem, **DOWN** from heaven came God's Spirit—

to fill them and empower them to carry on the

work of Jesus right across the world. In the **YEARS** and then

the **DECADES** afterward, the good news of Jesus SPREAD

and SPREAD. Men and women followed Jesus, just as

John had done, and churches sprang up nearly

EVERYWHERE. But some powerful people didn't like this. And it wasn't

long before Christians were **ARRESTED** and **IMPRISONED** and

KILLED for what they believed. Most of John's friends—his fellow disciples—

met that fate. And John himself was exiled to an island called Patmos, off the

coast of Greece. Then, amazingly, miraculously, John saw

Jesus again! It was in a **VISION** this time—a vision

filled with strange pictures of what God had done and

was doing and was going to do. John wrote it all down. We call it the book of

REVELATION. At the very end of that book, there is

a picture of what God has in store for the world and for

his people. "I saw a new heaven and a **NEW** earth,"

John says. "For the first heaven and the first earth had passed away. And

the seas with them. Then I saw a new Jerusalem too, coming **DOWN** from

heaven. And it was as **BEAUTIFUL** as a bride ready to meet her husband. I

heard a voice next, a voice from the throne of God. '**LOOK!**' the

voice said. 'God will make his home with women and with men. He will live with

them. He will be their God and they will be his people. He will wipe the

tears from their eyes. For there will be no more death. That's right!

And no more mourning, either. And CRYING and PAIN? Their day will be

over. For all that once was will disappear and God will make everything

new!'" And there will be more, so much more...

FOR-EVER!

Bob Hartman has an international reputation as a storyteller and writer. He has entertained audiences on both sides of the Atlantic, including performances at the Edinburgh International Book Festival and Northern Children's Book Festival. Bob is the author of more than 70 books for children, including the bestselling *The Lion Storyteller Bible*. He has also written the stories in YouVersion's Bible App for Kids, which has been downloaded over 35 million times and is available in 50 languages. Born in the USA, Bob now lives in Wiltshire.

Gareth Williams is an illustrator and designer living in South Wales. He studied Illustration at Swansea Metropolitan and since then has worked with leading stationery and greeting cards companies. His work has a strong illustrative influence, with lots of textures and layers to create a hand-drawn style.